tamryn kirby's
Wedding
SECRETS

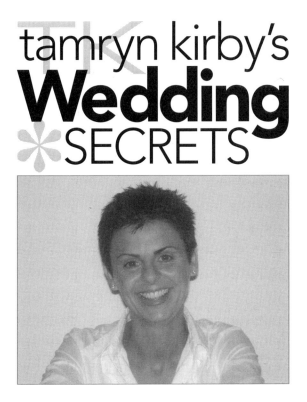

LONDON  YDNEY

D0265874

foulsham

The Publishing House, Bennetts Close, Cippenham,
Slough, Berkshire, SL1 5AP, England

Foulsham books can be found in all good bookshops and direct
from www.foulsham.com

ISBN 13: 978-0-572-03217-3
ISBN 10: 0-572-03217-X

Copyright © 2006 Tamryn Kirby

Main cover picture © Superstock

Additional pictures © TK Weddings

A CIP record for this book is available from the British Library

The moral right of the author has been asserted

While every effort has been made to ensure the
accuracy of all the information contained within this
book, neither the author nor the publisher can be
liable for any errors. In particular, since laws change
from time to time, it is vital that each individual checks
relevant legal details for themselves.

Neither the editors of W. Foulsham & Co. Ltd nor the
author nor the publisher take responsibility for any
possible consequences from any procedure or action
by any person reading or following the information in
this book.

Printed in Great Britain by St. Edmundsbury Press, Bury St. Edmunds, Suffolk

Contents

One
It's Your Wedding

If you have picked this book up, then it's highly likely that you're either planning your own wedding or helping someone who is planning theirs, so congratulations and welcome to the amazing experience that is wedding preparation! It can be undeniably fun and wonderfully emotional but sometimes confusing and stress inducing. So whilst it's only natural to be terribly excited about the task ahead, it's just as understandable to be slightly anxious because planning a wedding is a mammoth task.

On average, it takes a couple more than 250 hours to finalise all the arrangements for their big day. Not only do you have to find all this extra time in your life, you also have to set budgets, deal with family politics, make huge decisions and deal with any number of tiny details. When you add to that the probability that your wedding will be the first big event that you have ever organised, it's already easy to understand why plenty of brides feel overwhelmed rather than over the moon during their engagement.

To help make sure that you get the unique, wonderful wedding that you want, this book is here to help you every step of the way, whether you are just about to set a date or even if you are days away from the big 'I will'. There is clear and practical information on setting a budget, helpful tips for when you are visiting venues or selecting suppliers, dos and don'ts for dress shopping, beauty hints for perfect photos, delectable design details and advice on etiquette and common dilemmas, as well as endless little reminders and notes that will make your wedding planning experience blissful rather than stressful. I'm going to try and pass on to you in this book as many tips and tricks as I can to share the knowledge that I've built up by working on over a hundred unique and wonderful weddings.

Do It Your Way

Despite what you will have heard from the wedding cynics, more and more couples are choosing to take the plunge every year, and to my mind, that is incredibly admirable. Without a doubt each and every bride and groom wants to stamp their personalities on their wedding, to make it their own day, to make it stand out, to make it a memorable celebration and, above all, to make it unique. In many ways, planning a wedding full of individual touches is easier now than ever before with the choice of ceremonies available, the variety of venues and the surplus of suppliers in the marketplace, but all these options can cause problems too. How do you know who is great and who is not? Will what you want to do actually work on the day? Will all your hard work be noticed and appreciated by your guests and how do you make your selections from the seemingly endless lists of ideas and products that are out there?

Additionally, in this atmosphere that encourages everyone to 'have their day their way', lots of couples are now choosing to omit certain 'traditions' from their wedding plans. This leaves the problem of how do you deal with comments from friends and family who are shocked when they find out you're not going to have a first dance, or that you have other plans for your bouquet than to toss it into the crowd at the end of the night. I hope that if you take one thing from this book that it will be the knowledge and courage that will enable you to plan the unique wedding you want, not the wedding you feel you should have. I can promise you that you will be immeasurably happier on your wedding day if you feel comfortable with the plans that you have made.

If you feel unhappy with any detail or aspect of the arrangements during the run-up to the day, that feeling won't change come the day itself, so don't put yourself under added pressure by trying to shoehorn yourselves into anything you don't feel at ease with. It is better in the long run to have a discussion when a situation arises, even if it's uncomfortable at the time, than to go along with something and become increasingly apprehensive as the months go by.

Some Preliminary Points

One myth I'd like to dispel right now is that you need a huge budget to be able to have a great wedding. That is simply not true because in many instances, it's the thought and personality that is put into the wedding rather than the number of cheques written that make the event. It's relatively easy to buy completely co-ordinating accessories from any number of sources but it doesn't cost a penny to sit down and think carefully about your hobbies, likes, family history and to find ways to incorporate pieces of you both into the day. And what will delight your guests? The details that could only belong to you both or the items that could belong to anybody? Except for a very few couples, everyone has to work to a budget with their wedding, so deciding on your priorities at the outset, managing your budget carefully, building in some contingency plans and not pushing yourselves to spend every last penny that you earn on your wedding is certainly the way forward.

There is plenty of budgeting information in Chapter 3 as well as ideas for making the most of your money. Sometimes, however, working with your budget rather than feeling constrained by it can have excellent results. If you simply don't have the money to fling at every part of your wedding (and despite how it might feel, sometimes, only a tiny minority of couples do!), then you need to think creatively about what you are going to include and how to create the maximum impact with the resources you have.

Once you've looked through wedding magazines, leafed through catalogues and browsed numerous on-line stores, it's quite likely that you'll feel you have to have everything otherwise your wedding will somehow be lacking and not as special as others. That's certainly not the case and, in many instances, less really is more. If you cram your tables with every kind of decoration available at huge cost, will it look better? Will there be more of a wow factor for your guests? It's unlikely because it's been proven that humans can only take in a limited number of details from each view at one time and even if we try really hard, our memories can only retain a certain number of images. Limiting the detail actually creates more of an impact because guests are able to focus on and appreciate every item. If you think carefully about where each special touch is situated within the day, it can appear to your guests as if the day is nothing but an endless ribbon of perfect details.

The wedding industry in the UK has grown hugely over the past few years, which means that the variety of suppliers in the marketplace is now absolutely astounding. Of course it is in their interests to make you feel that the success of your wedding somehow rests on their product. Try to keep in mind that ultimately your guests are coming to your day to share the experience with you, not for anything else. If you have the budget for fancy favours, knockout entertainment and a free bar then that's great but if you haven't, so what? Your guests will accept your invitation because, above all, they want to see you get married and be a part of your day. Their attendance does not depend on what has been arranged for them. Of course, it's great to treat your guests and host a fabulous day but that isn't achieved simply by throwing money at things.

The best weddings are those where the details are well thought out and the wedding is a perfect fit for the couple involved regardless of what has been spent. A wedding with a happy bride and groom, who are relaxed and loving every moment of the day, is always going to be more enjoyable for guests than one where the wedding party is tense and uptight. Ideally, you want to wave goodbye to your guests at the end of the event with them all saying 'this wedding could only have been yours' because that's what will make it a wonderfully memorable occasion and a budget doesn't have to play a part in that – your thoughtfulness and attitude does.

Dip into this Book for Inspiration

Now all that sounds simple and it can be if you use the advice in this book. There is no need to sit and studiously read each page if you don't want to because it's just as easy to dip into each chapter when you need more information, a few ideas, some great tips or just a little reassurance. This is simply your starting point because everything contained in the following chapters can be adapted to suit your wedding, budget, situation and likes and dislikes. You can pick and choose pointers that appeal to you and you can disregard information on traditions or items that don't interest you at all.

I'm not going to tell you what you have to do and what you have to have because the great thing about weddings is that there is no set 'how to' list, no ultimate formula and no manual from which you must never deviate. Although that might initially seem scary, once you learn how to work with your personalities, focus on what you really want and gain the confidence to say no to things you don't, it is incredibly empowering. Of course, when you reach the big day and are surrounded by all the people you love most in the world, it will be an indescribable feeling that will stay with you for many years to come.

Two
Your Wedding Ideas

It is quite possible that as soon as you hear the words 'will you marry me?' that you will begin to get lots of ideas about your dream wedding day in your head. Actually, it wouldn't be surprising if some of those images had been there for quite a few years and, with the emergence of the engagement ring, they've started to run riot! Now is the moment to start to make those thoughts real, to look at your priorities and to gather inspiration and ideas.

Most of all, now is the time to start to deal with everyone else's expectations of your wedding as well. This probably doesn't seem like the most enjoyable start to your wedding planning but it's certainly easier to set these guidelines early on in the organisational process. That way you don't have to deal with awkward moments months down the line. By then people may have made up their own minds as to what you should be including and who you should be inviting and where you should be celebrating.

Brainstorming Basics

One of the most important things to remember during the entire planning process is actually also one of the hardest to achieve. You have to keep in your mind that the wedding is about two people; it's not just the result of one person's work. As difficult as it might be, your fiancé needs to have his input into the day as well. It's true that the vast majority of men will not have any interest in the thickness of ribbon to be tied around favour boxes or the number of votives on each table at dinner but there are areas to which he will want to contribute. Therefore sit down together at a very early point and ask your man exactly what areas of the planning he does want to be involved in so you know where you stand over the coming months. Whilst it's unlikely that he will have strong views on the size of the font in the orders of service, or the pens you provide for the signing of the guest book, it is highly possible that he will have some thoughts on the 'bigger' parts of the day and all those thoughts deserve to be heard.

TAMRYN'S TIP

Put a time limit on your early brainstorming sessions. Say to your husband-to-be 'let's just sit down for an hour and get through as much as we can and then we can do something else.' You're more likely to get total concentration from your man if the discussion is focused and there's an end in sight!

At this point, you don't need to be wading through endless stacks of wedding magazines and trying to decide on the minutiae, however appealing they may seem. At this point, you do need to be discussing your overall thoughts for the occasion, things that you think are the most important and maybe even the people you want to be involved. You don't even need to decide upon a budget now because until you're certain of what you both want, what your priorities and your 'optional extras' are, you can't begin to apportion your funds accordingly anyway.

It's always wise to take notes of your thoughts and ideas when you're brainstorming because you might well want to come back to a suggestion or idea at a later date. You will also probably need these notes when you're looking at venues or trying to set a date. So, with your notebook or laptop by your side, the following areas are those you need to discuss before you can really start planning your wedding.

Type of Marriage Ceremony

This is something you do need to talk about sooner rather than later. Of course you might already know you'll be having a religious or civil wedding ceremony but if you don't, you both need to come to a joint decision because it's the one decision that will have the biggest impact on the day you plan, and rightly so because as lovely as the party is to arrange, it's the ceremony itself that is the focus of the day.

If you're unsure of the requirements and workings of each variety of ceremony, then flick to Chapter 4. However, here are some things to get you thinking if you are still unsure – do you have an affiliation with any church? Are you looking to get married away from your home area? Does the prospect of a traditional day appeal to you or does the prospect of getting married in a country house, castle or another unusual venue seem more inviting?

Don't rush this discussion; listen to what you both want and try to reach a decision that you're both happy with.

Intimate or Super-sized?

There's no need to start writing your guest list at this stage but it's helpful to come to an agreement regarding the rough size of the wedding quite early on because obviously the number of people that you are intending to invite will have numerous knock-on effects. There's no right or wrong size for a wedding because some people love the prospect of a gigantic celebration, whilst others are drawn to a more intimate gathering.

It is true, in some respects, that each additional guest incurs additional costs. However, it's certainly possible to provide for a large number of people on any budget but you may have to trade a stunning venue with higher usage fees against increased catering costs. The size of your respective families and numbers of friends will naturally play a part here. Remember you don't need to invite everyone to the entire day, as some people could simply be included on the guest list for the evening reception. You will still need to have a rough idea of numbers in your head because, as we'll see in Chapter 5, venues have to place restrictions on numbers of people for health and safety reasons.

Spring, Summer, Autumn, Winter

You've not got around to setting a firm date yet but is there a season that you'd particularly like to get married in? It's always worth keeping in mind that summer dates are very popular, venues and suppliers get booked years in advance and lots of people take holidays at this time. This means that you will either need slightly longer to plan a summer wedding or you will have to be a little more flexible on dates and locations if you're not prepared to wait a few years.

Winter weddings are becoming increasingly popular with couples who are drawn to the prospect of mulled wine and roaring log fires, but of course lots of venues are often booked with Christmas parties so availability can often be as limited as in summer. Spring weddings, particularly those around Easter time, can be brilliant but you do need to have contingency plans for those spring showers! Autumn is often the 'quiet' time of the wedding season. If you don't want to be planning for a long time, looking at an autumnal date is often a wise idea.

Priorities

It's an undeniable fact that every couple will have different priorities for their wedding day and it is crucial that you know what yours are before you start allocating your budget to various elements of the day. Do you want a really amazing venue? Are you not that bothered about spending a large amount of your cash on a live band when you know what you really want is plenty of good food? Have you always dreamt of a handmade wedding dress but have not once thought about vintage cars? Discussing and recording your thoughts on all of these things will help you decide on your priorities. List things such as the venue, food, drink, flowers, entertainment, cars, clothing, cake, photos and video and rate their importance to you both. I would suggest, however, that photography is one of your priorities as your wedding photos will be your permanent reminder of your wedding day. There is more information in Chapter 12 about how to go about choosing the best photographer for you.

Your Ideal Day

This is the time to start allowing your creativity to go crazy and this in turn is where you can start coming up with ideas and inspiration for your wedding. What would be your ideal wedding day? Start talking about everything you'd like, describe what you see in your mind when you think about your wedding and, again, make as many notes as you can.

Perhaps you should both write down the five words that you'd use to describe your dream day and see what the similarities are. Have you both said 'relaxed', 'elegant', 'fun' or something else entirely? The words that you've used will give you a big clue to the style of day that will suit you both. For example, if you've said 'relaxed' then you won't want to be working to rigid timescales throughout the day, while a 'fun' wedding probably won't involve hours spent having endless formal photographs taken, so use these words to help define your wedding.

Lots of the things that you talk about at this point might not be of use until you are further down the planning path but it's very helpful to record everything now. Being able to refer back to these things will help to keep you on track to get the wedding that you both want.

At these early brainstorming sessions, remember that there's no correct answer, nothing has to be done or included simply because it's been mentioned once and, of course, you can change your mind on some things when you start investigating them more. However, these discussions are a great starting point and they allow you to get all of your ideas out into the open.

Being Inspired . . .

Once you've had a few of these preliminary planning conversations, I'm sure you'll start to have a slightly clearer image in your head about your wedding day so now is the time to start hunting around for some inspiration which will help you refine these ideas even further.

There are plenty of ways to help you kickstart your creativity. Note what styles, colours and ideas you always seem to be drawn to as you go. Buy a few wedding magazines and read through them, ripping out any images you like and even those that you don't because both are just as helpful. Even if you're not totally sure about what you'd like, if you're certain about what you don't, it's just as good a place to start! Spend some time browsing on the internet at some of the big wedding websites – are there any ideas on them that appeal to you? If so, note them down or print off the relevant page.

Perhaps visit a wedding fair or two and see what suppliers you relate to – do you feel more comfortable with solid and incredibly experienced suppliers or are you happier with younger, more creative companies? Collect a few business cards and leaflets from people you like because it will save you time in the future. Speak to any friends who are recently married or take a look on some internet wedding chat forums – what do the newlyweds count as money well spent or money wasted? What did their guests really appreciate and what wasn't noticed?

Your Ideas File

With all this research, begin to put together a file of your ideas which will start to show quite clearly what you like and what you don't! This file is great to take to meetings with potential suppliers and it's also very handy to use when you are starting to research people such as florists and photographers – does their style match with the style of your ideas? A great wedding is one where you're on the same wavelength as your suppliers. This allows you to relax because you are confident that you are going to get what you want and it allows your suppliers to work in the style that suits them best, which is when you're guaranteed to get great results.

Keep in mind that your ideas file is just that – ideas. It's not a definitive shopping list of everything you have to have or can only have. It is a starting point, not the finished article. It's helpful to have images of the following in your ideas file:

* Bride's dress
* Bridesmaid dress(es)
* Men's suits
* Shoes and accessories
* Bouquets
* Buttonholes
* Table centres
* Other decorations
* Cakes
* Little details such as favours, place cards, table plans, stationery

It's also a sensible idea to keep any 'real-life wedding' photos from magazines if you particularly like the way a certain moment has been captured. This is helpful when you're looking for a photographer because you will know if black and white photos are more appealing to you than colour and if you prefer posed or spontaneous photography. There is such a wide choice available to you for everything wedding related that having a starting point when you're searching will really save you time as you will have a clearer understanding of what you want and what you like.

Getting Everyone Involved

It goes without saying that your wedding day needs to be just that, *your* wedding day. It should be an expression of you both, your style, your likes and dislikes and you should be surrounded by all the people you want to share this great day with. However, weddings are undeniably family occasions and lots of your closest relatives will probably want to get involved in the planning as well.

So how do you manage to bring people into the excitement of the arrangements and still retain control when you're being faced with a seemingly endless stream of suggestions and comments? It's not an easy task and if you're finding it tough, you're not alone! Of the hundreds of e-mails and phone calls that I receive from clients every year, a great proportion of them are to do with family problems, which is a shame because a wedding can give everyone a chance to spend time together working towards a shared goal.

In my experience, the key to keeping relations sweet in the build-up to the day is to be clear with everyone from the outset. I don't mean that you need to be blunt or harsh with anyone but I do mean that you need to be firm and consistent in what you are telling and asking people.

Dealing with the First Questions

Once you and your partner have had a few of the basic brainstorming sessions mentioned earlier in this chapter, you'll have a reasonably good idea of the outline structure for the day and this will help you to deal with the first questions that are fired at you! So when you are asked when the wedding will be or who will be invited, you can state 'we've discussed this together and we've decided on an intimate spring wedding/ large winter wedding' or whatever it is you've gone for.

When you state everything firmly, people soon get the message that there's no room for interference but if you say 'well, I think...' in answer to any question, it sounds as though there's always the chance you could be persuaded to another way of thinking! Plus, by reiterating that every decision was a joint one, you sound even stronger.

There's no need to feel that you need to provide specifics at this point and if you feel you're getting pushed, don't feel bad about pointing out that you are still newly engaged and you're enjoying that feeling without needing to rush headlong into planning – although it might be an idea to hide your ever-expanding ideas file when you make that comment!

Expanded Brainstorming

Including your family in the ideas and inspiration stage can really help too. Once you start talking together and bouncing suggestions around, things tend to develop more quickly and there are other people to provide objective opinions on ideas as well. The following suggestions might help make these discussions go more smoothly.

* Only offer options that you like – if you know you really want a high summer wedding, ask whether people feel July or August would be better. If you simply ask which month might be a good choice, you'll be discussing Christmas weddings before you can say 'I will'.

* Be clear that this is an ideas session and explain that you both want to go away and talk about the suggestions that were made before you jointly make a final decision. Point out that you want to make sure that your final choice is right for you both and that you don't feel that anything about marriage and weddings should be rushed into.

* Even if you're almost having to sit on your hands to stop yourself from grabbing the car keys and heading straight to the nearest dress shop to try on some gowns, it's important to understand that you do need to consider things carefully before committing, especially with regard to parents and relatives. It's easy to say to your partner 'I think I've changed my mind about this' but when you're having to make the same explanation to more people, it gets much harder and this is when people can start to become defensive.

TAMRYN'S TIP

If you feel that discussing wedding arrangements with your family might be a little stressful, how about going out to do it? Sometimes talking in a neutral location can be easier and if you go out for dinner or a drink, it feels more relaxing and special.

✳ Don't build-up other people's expectations unnecessarily. It may be tempting to enthuse over ideas that you're not keen on to please other people. Although this initially seems like a good idea, there will come a point when it's clear that you didn't like that suggestion and won't be including it in the day. It is better to pass over a comment early on than appear to love it only to drop it later, by which time it will be much harder to do.

CHAPTER CHECKLIST

After reading this chapter and having embarked on a little brainstorming and ideas gathering, you should be able to tick the following from your wedding 'to do' list:

✳ The type of wedding ceremony, the approximate size of the wedding and the season in which the wedding will be held.

✳ Have a clear understanding of your joint priorities for the wedding day and understand what is less important to you both.

✳ Begin to put together an ideas file including your early thoughts on the day and images that you like and don't like.

✳ Start to notice suggestions and styles that keep recurring in your brainstorming and ideas file.

✳ Involve others in the early planning stage but remember to be firm and fair!

Three
First Things First

Before you can launch yourself headlong into planning your wedding, there are a few things that need to be arranged at the outset as they will literally dictate everything – the date, the ceremony, the budget and the number of guests you hope to invite. You also need to get yourself organised early on because staying on top of letters, brochures, e-mails and invoices is the best way to keep yourself sane. I'm not going to pretend that discussing money and working out a filing system for quotes, contracts and invoices are the best bits of wedding planning but I can state quite confidently that they are essential. If you can finalise these points early on, you can get on with enjoying the rest of the process knowing exactly where you stand and what needs to be done.

Setting a Date

After your brainstorming sessions, you'll probably have a reasonably clear idea of when in the year you would like your wedding to take place. Saturday nuptials are still the most popular but an increasing number of couples are choosing to say 'I will' on Friday and Sundays and, in particular, Sundays that fall before a Bank Holiday Monday. A few years ago, you could have landed yourself some great discounts for weddings on either Sundays or Fridays but that's not so much the case now as these days are becoming more commonplace. Likewise, 'off-season' discounts for winter weddings are dwindling too because, for the majority of suppliers, the wedding season runs for a complete year and isn't just confined to summer months. You might be able to pick up a bargain but don't choose your date solely based on the hope of getting a few discounts.

Lots of couples choose dates that are important to them or to other family members such as using the date of their grandparents' wedding anniversary. Others, very practically, plump for a date just after pay day, one that fits around work and any other commitments or one that allows them to visit their dream honeymoon destination at the best time of year. Some even check the availability of their dream venue first! However, the majority of couples just decide on a date for no other reason than it's in front of them when they flick through their diary and there is absolutely nothing wrong with that at all.

TAMRYN'S TIP

If you are very sure of the people you want to include in the wedding party, it might be a good idea to double-check they don't have a holiday booked for the date you want. It's easy to pick another date but not to replace a dear friend or family member.

Type of Ceremony

Again, this is a very personal decision and not one that anyone can make for you. Obviously, if you've been brought up in a particular faith, then it is very likely you will marry in your church. If, however, you are less religious, been married before, are of mixed faith or you simply don't feel that a church wedding is right for you, a civil ceremony would probably be more appropriate.

Civil ceremonies were once seen as the 'poor relation' of a church wedding as sometimes register offices can seem a little bland. However, with the emergence of 'approved venues', civil ceremonies can now take place in castles, stately homes, country hotels and more obscure and unusual venues such as museums. A large number of register offices have undergone a makeover and lots are housed in historic civic buildings. If you are on a really tight budget, a register office wedding does work out to be the cheapest option and the solemn and binding vows that you make there are just as meaningful and just as legal as those you would make in a cathedral or castle.

There's much more information about the legal requirements for wedding ceremonies in Chapter 4, and a rundown on the associated costs but of all the decisions you make about your wedding, this certainly needs to be the one that you are both totally comfortable with. You can live with the music to your first dance that your partner has chosen and they can go along with your choice of place card but it's less likely that you could go along with a ceremony you're not happy with – and neither should you have to. Take time to discuss your options if you are not immediately drawn to one variety, talk about your feelings regarding a church or civil ceremony and then the final decision should be one that you are both happy with.

Setting a Budget

Talking about money is never easy and to make it that much harder, there is really no right way to work at setting your budget. Everyone has different incomes, different attitudes to spending money on their wedding day and, of course, different offers of financial help from families. A good way to start is to make a list of everything you might need for the day and to write a rough cost next to it. Mark things that are your priorities – for example, you might be willing to forego massive fresh flower arrangements so that you can have a live band in the evening, or you may feel that having fabulous photographs is more important than providing limitless alcohol to your guests. To give you a rough guide of the various costs involved, everything is listed below for you. Of course, the only part of the day you really need is the ceremony, anything after that point is a bonus.

TAMRYN'S TIP

Remember that costs only ever go up – not down – and any figures given in this chapter are rough guides only based on figures released in 2006.

The Ceremony

A marriage in a register office will cost under £100 but a wedding at an approved premises will cost more as the registrar will make an extra charge to attend. This fee varies but is usually in the region of £200. You will also need to pay any charge the venue makes for a ceremony to be held there and also the £30 each to give notice and the £3.50 for your marriage certificate. Check with your local office as to what their charges are. Church ceremony costs can vary and 'donations' can often match fees at an approved venue. Adding in choirs and bellringers increases the cost, although charges for these vary from church to church.

Wedding Rings

An average figure would be £400 for both. However, you can buy gold bands for much less and heavy platinum bands for much more so you need to decide what you want before you can set a budget.

Outfits

The current average for a bridal gown is £900, but a dress from the high street will be more in the £300 area while a designer dress could cost thousands. Shoes and other accessories can add another £300 but the groom gets away quite lightly here – the hire of outfits is often less than £100 per person and lots of stores run a 'hire four and the groom goes free' promotion. Bridesmaids' dresses start at under £100 for something off the peg from a department store and increase in price for specially designed dresses. About £250 is a good guide for a dress from a wedding shop. You then need to add around £150 for a bridesmaid's shoes and accessories. A bride will often spend around £100 on underwear for the day and another £150 on make-up and skincare. Obviously if you're planning on a course of facials, manicures and haircuts, this will add quite a bit. Of course, this is an area where you can make some savings – ditch the designer shoes for a more affordable pair and you can really start to trim your spending.

Photographs

Unless you have a friend who will take your photos for free, you will need a professional. A traditional posed album will be roughly £500 while a good-quality reportage album will start at around the £1,000 mark.

Videos

Expect to pay in the region of £500 for a videographer but 'extras' such as DVDs or fancy editing are likely to add to that cost. Of course, if you have a friend with a camera and tripod, you can get footage of the ceremony for free!

Flowers

This is an area that can dramatically alter your budget, especially if you want masses of blooms. The bridal bouquet costs roughly £100, each bridesmaid's bouquet is in the region of £50 and buttonholes are around £5 each. An average cost of venue flowers is around £250. See Chapter 14 for ideas on how to use your floral cash.

Transport
Wedding cars will cost in the region of £400, but if you're looking for something ultra-flash or will be providing transport for everyone, add another couple of hundred pounds to that figure. At the other end of the scale, you can use a friend's car for free or hire an 'executive' car by the hour for less than £100.

Stationery
You'll probably end up spending around £200 on wedding stationery. You can pay less if you buy pre-printed from the high street or make your own and you can pay much more if you want high-quality traditional styles.

The Venue
Average venue hire charges will add up to around £1,000. Be sure to check the small print with regards to room hire, late licence fees and insurance before you sign a contract as these can add £100s to what appeared to be a very reasonable quote. There are plenty of options open to you, however, right through from a village hall to exclusive weekend use of a country property. See Chapter 5 for more venue information.

Food, Drink and the Wedding Cake
Apparently, the 'average' couple pays over £2,300 for food at their reception and almost another £1,000 on drinks and champagne. Food and drink is something on which you can spend as much or as little as you like; it just depends what you decide to provide. A traditional three-tier fruit wedding cake will be around £250, but for a more unusual creation expect to pay around £500. From these figures, the cost of feeding and watering a guest works out as an average of £45 per head. You can spend more or less it depends on your priorities.

The Party

Entertainments will often add around £700 to your budget, maybe less for a DJ and often more for a band. If you add ceremony musicians into the equation, you need to add another £400 to that. If you are planning on giving favours, they can add around £100 and balloon decorations are usually another £150. Thank-you gifts to the wedding party are currently averaging a total of £200.

Going Far, Far Away...

For most couples, the honeymoon is one of the major expenses. Again, the 'average' is over £2,500 but you'd be looking at almost £5,000 for two weeks in a top-class hotel, more if you want to upgrade your flights. Conversely, a romantic cottage holiday in the UK would be around £500 for a week including food, while a last-minute package could get you your dream destination for a fraction of the advertised costs. The 'first night' is legendary and an average of £150 is spent on a suitably wonderful hotel room. Even brides not leaving the reception as tradition dictates will still spend an average of £150 on a 'going away' outfit, which is often just a smart travelling outfit or a funky personalised T-shirt with designer jeans and boots.

Organising Your Budget

Now that you've read all that, you're probably feeling that setting a budget might not be the most exciting wedding-related task but it is very important. Getting carried away on a few items early on and then running out of funds before the day can be heartbreaking so it's best to be careful from the outset. One of the best things you can do when you've worked out the figure that you can afford for your wedding is not to plan to spend every penny. Say, for example, that your absolute maximum spend is £12,000, then you should aim to only spend £10,800 which leaves you 10 per cent for emergencies. If this cash is still free nearer the time, use it to upgrade your honeymoon, splash out on a few more flowers or bottles of champagne – or bank it for something else. However, if as you're going along, a photographer you love costs a little more than your predictions, you can still book them without having to trim costs elsewhere. By doing this, you'll save yourself lots of nightmares and if an unexpected cost crops up, you will not be left reeling.

Another thing you must do is ensure that you get all quotations in writing so that they are legally binding. This makes things a little easier to deal with if a supplier tries to overcharge you at a later date or change what's included in the price you've been given. The quotation should be as detailed as possible so you can be sure of exactly what you'll receive for your money. It should also detail dates that payments are due to be made, forms of payment that are acceptable and any other related terms and conditions. Do always read them carefully before you agree to a quote and always keep copies in your wedding file. You should also add all invoices, receipts and bills to your file and note dates when you've made payments. In short, keep all communications from your suppliers as you never know when you might need to refer to them.

Sticking to Your Budget

One key thing to remember throughout is that budgets are supposed to be finite so if you can't afford four bridesmaids and the honeymoon you want, you'll have to consider making a few changes to suit your purse. It's better to do this earlier rather than later and risk upsetting or disappointing yourself or others. If there's something you think that you really, really want, you'll have to decide where to make sacrifices in order to make it happen.

Please, don't get carried away with believing that everything is essential and remember that it's not called 'the wedding industry' for nothing! There are literally thousands of companies out there who sell everything and anything that's wedding related. You might not have even thought about engraved wedding rings or hand-etched candles but someone somewhere will try to sell them to you. If something is not in your original budget, you need to think about the impact it will have on the other things that you have planned before you add a new item to the list.

Open a Wedding Account

In the same spirit of organisation and clarity, you might want to open a special wedding bank account so that cheques or payments aren't coming from your personal accounts. This makes it clear how much you have left or how much you need to find. Also, if you have any generous relatives or if you're squirreling money away yourself, it makes sure that these additional contributions don't end up in the joint account paying for food or petrol. It can be very satisfying to see that pot of money building up over time.

A good budget spreadsheet will help you keep track of payments you've made and those that are still outstanding. Noting everything in one place will allow you to see at a glance the exact status of your wedding finances and although it might not make comfortable viewing at times, I really would encourage you to include as much as possible on your spreadsheet. It's very easy to make a few 'little' purchases that add up and all of a sudden start eating into your available funds. Be strict with yourself, because I can promise you it will stop you worrying about money closer to the wedding when you will rightly want to have other things on your mind! To make it even easier for you, there's a budget spreadsheet at the end of this chapter for you.

TAMRYN'S TIP

When you see something new that you suddenly think you must have for the day, don't order it immediately. Make yourself wait two weeks and, at the end of this time, if you still think it's necessary, you know how you can use it AND you have the money for it, then go ahead. Don't let yourself get swept along in the excitement and find you end up with less money and more items than you can use.

How to Pay for It All

Clearly, at some point, you've got to pay for your wedding and there are a few options that are open to you. Whatever you decide, make sure you can afford it first. Starting married life with debt hanging over you and having to make monthly repayments for years to come isn't wildly romantic, however fabulous your day was. However, as with all things relating to your wedding, that's a decision that only you can make, but I would encourage you to get some independent financial advice before you commit to anything long-term. Here are some ways to pay and things to consider.

Saving

You can decide to save a certain amount per month that will cover everything that you plan to spend. It's a good idea to put this into a separate account so you're not tempted to blow it!

Credit Cards

You can pay for some things on your card (and for some purchases like rings and honeymoons this is a good idea as you're then covered by insurance protection offered by your card company). However, this will increase the amount you need to repay monthly and decrease the credit available on your card so think carefully about this. After the wedding you might like to think about transferring the balance to a low-rate card to cut down the payments.

Loan

If interest rates are low, a loan can seem like a good idea. If the monthly repayments are within your budget, you may want to consider a loan to get the day of your dreams, but the regular payments will hang over you for some time to come. Likewise, if you're thinking about moving house or starting a family in the near future, you need to be sure that even with a reduced income you can still make the repayments.

Re-mortgaging

If you've owned your own home for a while, the chances are that there is equity in it. If you can release this by re-mortgaging you can benefit. If your mortgage lender has you in a lock-in period, you might not be able to do this, but if you can, the amount added onto your repayments over 20 or so years is likely to be less than taking out a loan or increasing any credit card debt. As with a loan, this decision will have long-term repercussions for you both, so isn't to be taken lightly.

Be Realistic

It is very easy when you are browsing through wedding magazines and researching on-line to become fixated on the amounts that people have available to spend on their wedding day. However, a more realistic way to look at it is not simply as a final figure but rather as a percentage of your joint annual income. Regardless of the total cash that has been spent, it seems that most couples spend around 20 per cent of their joint annual income on their wedding. The most important thing is that it's an amount you can afford, you are comfortable spending and a total you've both agreed on. After that point, your budget isn't anyone else's business.

Organising Yourself

Getting and staying organised is the key to managing your stress levels in the build-up to your wedding and you should start as you mean to go on! You will know whether you're a paper- or PC-kind of person and you should certainly use whichever method you prefer for record keeping.

A good way to start would be to use the chapter titles of this book as the subject headings for each section of your system. Have one master sheet including confirmed details such as your venue address, ceremony time, members of the bridal party, suppliers, guest numbers etc., at the front of the file along with a budget spreadsheet. You can then see at a glance what has been paid for and what balances are still outstanding without having to rifle through your file to find paperwork in each section.

TAMRYN'S TIP

If you do any of your planning on your PC (guest list tracking, table planning, etc.), do make sure that you regularly back-up your files in case of a virus or file corruption. Losing lots of information isn't going to be good for your stress levels!

Each section of your file should include the following:

* Contracts with chosen suppliers.
* Invoices and/or receipts for any payments made.
* Copies of any correspondence discussing packages and prices.
* Information, brochures or catalogues sent to you by suppliers.

* Ideas or information that you have found online or in magazines.
* Your own personal notes, for example, ideas that you've had, contact details for potential suppliers or lists of questions you want to ask your venue.

Keep your file up-to-date with information and take it to all your final meetings closer to your wedding when you'll need to pass on your requests and other details to all your suppliers and to the organiser at your chosen ceremony and reception venues. Anything that you can do to keep yourself feeling organised and under control will help to lessen any 'out-of-control' feelings that can occur when you are further into the planning process.

CHAPTER CHECKLIST

Hopefully, with the help of this chapter, you will have worked your way through some of the least enjoyable aspects of wedding planning, especially the budgeting! So allow yourself a few moments of smugness because you've achieved the following:

* Set the date for your wedding celebrations.

* Made a final decision regarding the type of wedding ceremony you are going to have.

* Agreed a budget for the wedding day and noted your priorities so you know where you will be channelling your funds.

* Decided how you are going to fund the wedding and started to keep track of payments on your budget spreadsheet.

* Arranged your wedding file in a way that suits you so that everything is kept in one place and stress is kept at bay.

Wedding Budget Sheet

Our Wedding Budget is £ ....

Item	Estimated Cost	Actual Cost	Over or Under?
Press Announcements			
Engagement announcement			
Wedding announcement			
Engagement Party			
Venue			
Food			
Drink			
Entertainment			
Fees			
Giving notice			
Registrar fees for ceremony			
Venue fees for ceremony			
Marriage certificate			
Rings			
Engagement ring			
Groom's wedding ring			
Bride's wedding ring			
Bride			
Dress			
Shoes			
Veil			
Tiara or headdress			
Lingerie			
Jewellery			
Bag			
Make-up			

Who's Paying?	Deposit	Date Paid	Balance	When to Pay	Date Paid

Item	Estimated Cost	Actual Cost	Over or Under?
Hair			
Beauty treatments			
Going away outfit			
Groom			
Wedding outfit			
Shoes			
Going away outfit			
Barber			
Attendants' Outfits			
Adults' dresses			
Adults' shoes			
Adults' accessories			
Children's outfits			
Children's shoes			
Children's accessories			
Best Man outfit			
Usher outfit			
Fathers' outfits			
Photographs			
Package			
Extras			
Video			
Package			
Extras			
Flowers			
Bride's bouquet			
Bridesmaids' bouquets			
Buttonholes and corsages			

Who's Paying?	Deposit	Date Paid	Balance	When to Pay	Date Paid

Item	Estimated Cost	Actual Cost	Over or Under?
Ceremony room decorations			
Reception room decorations			
Car decorations			
Bouquets for mothers			
Transport			
Bride and father to ceremony			
Bride's mother and bridesmaids to ceremony			
Groom and best man to ceremony			
Bride and groom to reception			
Attendant and bride's parents to reception			
Other guests to reception			
Bride and groom from reception			
Stationery			
Invitations			
Postage			
Order of the day			
Menus			
Place cards			
Table plan			
Other stationery			
The Venue			
Room hire costs			
Late licence fee			

FIRST THINGS FIRST

Who's Paying?	Deposit	Date Paid	Balance	When to Pay	Date Paid

Item	Estimated Cost	Actual Cost	Over or Under?
Damage waiver			
Other insurances			
Other costs			
Food, Drink and Cake			
Celebration drinks after ceremony			
Meal			
Wine with meal			
Other drinks with meal			
Drinks for toasts			
Evening buffet			
Other drinks			
Other food			
Cakes			
The Party			
Band/DJ			
Ceremony music			
Favours			
Decorations			
Thank-you gifts			
Children's entertainments			
Fireworks			
Other entertainments			
Going Far, Far Away			
First night hotel			
Honeymoon			
Spending money			

FIRST THINGS FIRST

Who's Paying?	Deposit	Date Paid	Balance	When to Pay	Date Paid

Item	Estimated Cost	Actual Cost	Over or Under?
Wedding Insurance and Costs			
Wedding insurance			
Increasing home insurance			
Wedding co-ordinator			
Hen and Stag Nights			
Hen night			
Stag night			
Other Costs			
Fee to change name in passport			
TOTAL			

Who's Paying?	Deposit	Date Paid	Balance	When to Pay	Date Paid

Four
The Ceremony

There is no disputing the fact that the ceremony is the main focus of the day – it is the moment when you become husband and wife after all – and although it can be tempting to overlook this time in the rush and excitement of planning the smaller details, please keep in mind that without the marriage, there would be no wedding day. In this chapter are more details about civil, Church of England and Roman Catholic ceremonies as well as information on resources dealing with other denominational weddings. However, I can't stress enough that the best person to provide definitive information on all things concerning the marriage ceremony itself is the person who will be leading the event as he or she ultimately has control over how the service proceeds.

Whatever form of ceremony you opt for, remember that you must be happy with your choice. Don't feel pushed into a religious occasion because other people feel 'it is right', but don't deny yourself a spiritual ceremony if that's what you've always wanted and you feel making your vows in front of God is important to you. Conversely, don't opt for a church ceremony just for the 'pretty building' aspect of it as that does rather make a mockery of your marriage vows – standing in front of God on your wedding day should be done because you believe in Him, not because by doing that you can have photographs taken at a romantic-looking church. However, whatever ceremony you opt for, every ceremony is special and every occasion finishes with the same outcome – you and your partner become husband and wife.

Civil Ceremonies

Despite the fact that civil ceremonies can often be more flexible than religious ones in terms of location, music and readings, there are still rules that can't be broken. I will try to cover everything here but do please check things with your registrar before finalising any details, as each registrar interprets the law in different ways and what one will deem 'religious', another will accept.

Restrictions on Approved Premises

There are hundreds of approved premises across the UK, from stately homes to small hotels but each have to meet certain legal criteria. A venue must be open to the public so you cannot have a licence for a private residence. It must be 'suitably solemn' so a nightclub is out! It must also be 'fixed' so a ship could only qualify if it was moored permanently. It must also be indoors so a wedding cannot take place in the open air, although some venues with covered terraces or permanently fixed pergolas are licensed for ceremonies allowing couples to be outdoors, even if they have to be under cover for the legalities.

Dates

You can only officially set the date for a civil wedding one year in advance (when you 'give notice') and registrars will not make confirmed bookings before this point. However, it is at the registrar's discretion to make a provisional booking before the one-year deadline so that you can be sure someone will be available to marry you. You should call the registrar who will be carrying out your ceremony to find out if they will be willing to make a provisional booking for you. Having a provisional booking can be very helpful, especially when venues are booked so far in advance, as it's very reassuring to know that there will be someone to marry you at the time that you want! Don't forget to make an appointment with the appropriate register office to 'give notice' as soon as you are able to confirm your booking fully.

Legal Requirements to Marry

Whatever kind of ceremony you are having, you must meet the following legal requirements:

* ✳ You must be of different sexes.
* ✳ You must be over the age of 16 (but you will need written parental consent if you are under 18).
* ✳ You must be 'free to marry' which means you cannot be related.
* ✳ If you have been married before, you'll need to be able to prove that the marriage has ended (by Decree Absolute).
* ✳ You must also have two witnesses to your marriage ceremony (these can be decided much nearer the date if needs be).
* ✳ If you are gay or lesbian and want a civil partnership, look at www.opsi.gov.uk for the most up-to-date information with regards to the legalities.

Documents

When you visit the registrar to 'give notice', you'll need to take either a birth certificate or a passport as proof of identity. If you are under the age of 18, you'll need written consent from your parent or guardian. If you have been married before, you'll need to show either a Decree Absolute or the death certificate of your former spouse. These must all be the original documents, not copies.

Giving Notice

Firstly, call your local register office to make an appointment to give notice. Most only do this on certain days so it is best to call in advance. You must both go in person to the register office in your district (not the district in which you'll be marrying). You must have lived in this district for at least seven days before giving notice and you must give a minimum of 15 days, or a maximum of 12 months, notice of your intention to marry. The registrar will ask you a few questions about yourself and your partner and then your details will be entered into the marriage notice book. Notices of your proposed marriage are also displayed at the register office and this gives anyone who wishes to oppose your marriage 15 days to lodge a statement of objection. After the 15 days has passed, you can collect the certificates which allow your marriage to proceed. If a registrar from the office will be marrying you, simply leave the certificates with them. If you are marrying in another district, you will need to take your precious paperwork to the appropriate registrar at some point before the ceremony. The date of the marriage has to be within a year of giving notice otherwise you will have to go through the procedure again. The current fee for giving notice is £30 for the bride and £30 for the groom.

Meeting with the Registrar on the Day

Two registrars are present at a civil ceremony. The first will meet with you on the wedding day before the ceremony (you can make different arrangements if you would like to be interviewed separately) and most venues provide a room for this meeting to take place in. This interview is to go through the details that the registrar holds for you and to make any changes, such as a new address or age to ensure that the information entered onto your marriage certificate is correct. Some registrars conduct this interview before the wedding day to discuss readings and music, so do confirm whether or not you'll be speaking to the registrar prior to your ceremony. Registrars will also speak with your witnesses and readers just before the ceremony to confirm their names and their involvement in the event. The second registrar will sit in a corner of the ceremony room filling in the appropriate paperwork.

Witnesses

You must have two witnesses to your civil marriage. There is no set age limit but witnesses must be able to understand the implications of the vows that they listen to (so a young child is not suitable). They must also be close enough to you during the ceremony to hear the words you speak to each other.

The Ceremony

To help you know what to expect during a civil ceremony, I've outlined the mechanics of it below. I've broken this section down into three areas – before, during and after.

Before

As mentioned previously, before the ceremony can take place both parties usually see the registrar to confirm the details held in the marriage record book. Although this can seem slightly annoying when you're raring to go, it is important that these are correct as this information will be copied onto your marriage certificate once the deed is done! It's also a great opportunity to collect your thoughts and steady your nerves before you make your way into the ceremony room. You can arrange to be interviewed separately so that the groom goes first before making his way to the ceremony room to take his place at the front. The bride is then interviewed before proceeding to make her grand entrance!

During

Once the bride has joined her groom, the registrar will start the ceremony. He or she will usually make a few opening remarks to welcome the guests (and to give the couple time to relax) before starting the 'legal' part of the ceremony. The registrar will begin stating that you are in a place sanctioned for marriage and will then ask if anyone wishes to declare an objection. Once that moment is over (I can guarantee you'll be holding your breath at that point!), the registrar will remind you both of the 'solemn and binding character of the ceremony of marriage' before asking you to make your declarations to each other. This is the part where you say 'I do solemnly declare that I know not of any lawful impediment why I may not be joined in matrimony to …'. You both repeat these lines in turn, after the registrar, adding your names. Don't worry about forgetting the words as the registrar will only read small sections at a time and will prompt you if you need assistance.

TAMRYN'S TIP

It's very tempting, especially when you're feeling a little nervous, to look at the registrar when you are repeating your vows. Do try to avoid this and try to focus on your partner as the moment is more meaningful if you feel that you are speaking directly to your partner.

It is then time to contract the marriage – both of you will repeat 'I call upon these persons here present to witness that I do take thee to be my lawful wedded wife/husband'. You will probably be given a choice of words for the declaration and contracting words but you cannot add any of your own words to this part of the ceremony. However, you may add your own 'vows' to the ring exchange or you can use the words suggested by your registrar. The registrar then declares to everyone that you are married, the crowd go wild and you get to have your first married kiss! You both then need to sign the register along with your witnesses before the marriage certificate is completed. This can take a few minutes so some music at this point is a good way to fill any awkward silences. Once the certificate is completed and a copy handed to the newlyweds, the ceremony is over and you are free to make a big exit followed by your guests.

After

You are free to do what you like now and most couples opt for drinks and photographs before any food is served. How you structure the day from here is completely up to you, but whatever you do, you're now husband and wife!

Marriage Classes

For a Church of England ceremony and a Roman Catholic ceremony, most priests will insist that you both attend marriage preparation classes before your wedding. These are designed to encourage you to talk about your hopes for your marriage, what you think marriage is all about and the role of faith in your relationship. Some couples find the prospect of these classes scary but they are actually very enjoyable as you usually share the day with other couples so it's a great opportunity to meet some new people and discuss your wedding.

Church of England Ceremony

As marriage is a binding legal contract between two people, it is only right that there are some legal restrictions. I have tried to cover most points below but do check with your minister that you've done everything correctly!

Restrictions on Locations

In England, weddings must take place in a recognised religious building (unlike in Scotland), the doors must be unlocked at all times and the ceremony can take place at any time between 8am and 6pm. In theory, it can take place on any day but finding a vicar willing to perform a marriage during Christmas or Easter Day can be tricky.

Dates

As with civil ceremonies, you can only officially set the date for a wedding one year in advance. However, it is at the minister's discretion to make a provisional booking before the one-year deadline so that you can be sure someone will be available to marry you. Please call the officiant who would be carrying out your ceremony to find out if they would be willing to make a provisional booking for you.

Legal Requirements to Marry

The legal requirements are the same as those for a civil ceremony, so you must meet the following legal requirements:

* You must be of different sexes.
* You must be over the age of 16 (but you will need written parental consent if you are under 18).
* You must be 'free to marry' which means you cannot be related.

Documents

When you visit the minister to discuss your ceremony, you'll need to take either a birth certificate or a passport as proof of identification. If you are under the age of 18, you'll need written consent from your parent or guardian and if you've been married before, you'll need to show either a Decree Absolute or the death certificate of your former spouse. Most churches also require at least one person to produce their certificate of baptism, but do check this. All these must be original documents.

Witnesses

You must have two witnesses to your marriage. There is no set age limit but witnesses must be able to understand the implications of the vows that they listen to (so again a young child is not suitable). They must also be close enough to you during the ceremony to hear the words you speak to each other.

Obtaining Permission

There are various ways in which you can obtain religious permission to marry and I've detailed these in this section. Marriage by banns is the most common whilst marriage by special licence is really only for use in exceptional circumstances. Your minister will be able to give you more information should you need it and assist with your application if required.

Marriage by Banns

If one or both of you live in the parish where the ceremony will be held, your minister will read your banns on three Sundays before the wedding. The reading of the banns must be within three months of the date of the ceremony and most couples go to church on these days to hear their banns being read. This public declaration gives people the opportunity to raise any objections to your marriage as required by law. There is a fee to have your banns read (currently £15) and if you live in different parishes, you'll need to have your banns read there too (currently charged at £9) to obtain a banns certificate.

Marriage by Common Licence

This form of marriage is used when either the bride or groom is only resident in a parish temporarily (this must be 15 consecutive days before the licence can be granted). The minister involved will assist you in applying for the necessary licence and you'll be required to swear an affidavit (confirm your details) in the three-month period before your wedding. Common licences are not available to divorcees and one person must be baptised. There is also a fee for the common licence, which is £55 in 2006.

Marriage by Special Licence

This is granted by the Archbishop of Canterbury in exceptional circumstances only when marriage by banns or marriage by common licence cannot take place. You need to discuss your application with your minister and then the Faculty Office in London. There is a charge of £125.

The Ceremony

Once you have met all the church's requirements, you arrive at your wedding day and the ceremony itself. To help prepare you for the big moment, I have included a rundown of the usual format. However, your minister is likely to have talked to you at some length about the day by the time you reach this moment so you'll have a much clearer idea of what's going to happen before you reach the church door.

Before

Unlike a civil ceremony, the bride and groom do not need to see the vicar just before the ceremony to confirm their details. The bride arrives at the church and the processional music is played. The groom and best man take this as their sign to move to the top of the aisle and the entire congregation follows their lead and stands for the entrance of the bride. The bride makes her way down the aisle, holding her father's right arm. The chief bridesmaid, bridesmaids, flower girls or page boys follow. Traditionally, the bride's veil is lifted when she reaches her groom but who lifts the veil these days is up to the bride. Similarly, there's no requirement to have a veil simply because you are marrying in church. The bride's bouquet should also be handed to the chief bridesmaid.

During

Once the bride has joined her groom, the vicar will start the ceremony. He or she will usually make a few opening remarks to welcome the guests (and to give the bride and groom a few moments to relax) before the ceremony. Church ceremonies usually last at least 30 minutes (typically 40 minutes) but this obviously depends on the number of hymns and readings you have chosen. The words of the ceremony vary depending whether you choose the 1662, 1966 or 2000 version of the marriage ceremony. The 1662 ceremony is not often used these days as most couples prefer a ceremony that is more modern. Each ceremony starts with words regarding the significance of marriage before the minister asks the congregation if they know of any reason why the marriage should not go ahead. The bride and groom are both then asked if they are free to marry before being asked if they will marry each other! The vows are then made and the rings exchanged before the minister announces that the bride and groom are now husband and wife. The ceremony then includes hymns, readings or a sermon, ending with the signing of the register.

After

The bride takes her bouquet back from the chief bridesmaid and then takes her new husband's right arm to walk back down the aisle. They are followed by the chief bridesmaid and best man, the other attendants, the mother of the bride with the father of the groom and the groom's mother with the bride's father. Photographs are taken outside the church (and confetti thrown if allowed) before the bridal party departs.

Roman Catholic Ceremonies

Roman Catholic ceremonies are similar to the Church of England process as explained previously. However, there are a few differences to note.

Non-Catholics Marrying in a Catholic Church

If only one of you is of the Catholic faith, it's still possible for your marriage to take place in a Catholic church but you must usually agree that you will remain faithful to each other and expect to remain together for the rest of your lives, that you will have at least one child (if the bride is a suitable age) whom you will raise in the faith, and that you are marrying in the Church without any external pressure. The priest can then grant you 'Dispensation for a Mixed Marriage'. However, if one of you is not baptised, the Bishop will need to grant you 'Dispensation for Disparity of Cult'. Please allow sufficient time to arrange this if it is needed.

Weddings during Lent

Traditionally, weddings during Lent were not encouraged as this is a time of abstinence, not of feasting and celebration. Weddings during Lent should be without organ music and floral decorations but many priests will waive this rule. Nowadays, however, it is only ceremonies on the three days prior to Easter Sunday that are forbidden.

Nuptial Mass

A Nuptial Mass will usually include communion although this is not always the case with mixed-faith marriages. The ceremony will also include Bidding Prayers, which are short prayers read for the bride and groom wishing them well in their future together. These can be personally written or your priest can provide you with some standard wording.

Other Forms of Ceremony _____

Of course, there are many other forms of marriage ceremony: Jewish, Muslim, Hindu, Humanist and many more. For more information on these, please refer to the 'Further Information' chapter at the back of this book, which will give you details of groups and organisations that can provide you with information. A good place to start is always the officiant who will be leading the ceremony and who will be happy to talk to you about your plans and explain the requirements and format of the ceremony.

Music

The majority of couples use a combination of readings and pieces of music to personalise their ceremonies. Of course, there's no obligation to use either but both can enhance the occasion. The key is to try to use a combination of both and, as always, to keep it as personal and as meaningful as possible. If you need a little inspiration it might be worth reading *Wedding Readings & Musical Ideas* by Rev. John Wynburne and Alison Gibbs, also published by Foulsham.

Music is a fabulous way to make the ceremony come alive – it can be welcoming, joyous, celebratory and even a little humorous if you like!

If you're unsure of the classical music options, visit a local music store's classical section – there's always a number of CDs aimed at weddings that provide plenty of inspiration. Likewise, hunt around on the internet as there are a number of websites that will allow you to listen to excerpts of music so that you can make your choice and even download them if you want to make a compilation of your chosen tunes.

TAMRYN'S TIP

If you are playing a CD, enlist someone to be in charge of stopping and starting everything at the right moment. Ask them to experiment to find the right volume. Label the CDs to be used clearly and leave precise instructions on what is to be played and when.

Preludes

These are pieces that are played as the guests enter. Most people don't have exact choices for this section, instead they play a compilation of music, mainly instrumental, that just form a pleasant backdrop for guests. In a church ceremony, it is usually the organist who provides this music, while at a civil ceremony either a CD or live musicians will do the same job, depending on your budget.

The Processional

This is the piece that will be played when the bride makes her entrance. The pace of any music chosen for this section should be relatively steady so that it's easy for the bride to walk to without any sudden changes in tempo. Don't choose something too fast otherwise you'll feel the temptation to gallop up the aisle, while something too slow can appear a bit funereal. Favourite classical choices are 'Trumpet Voluntary' by Boyce, 'Prince of Denmark's March' by Clarke, 'Arrival of the Queen of Sheba' by Handel or a version of 'The Bridal March' by Parry or Wagner. If you fancy something a little more contemporary, maybe you could pick a song that was playing when you met or something that has a personal meaning.

Hymns

If you are having a religious ceremony and want your congregation to make some noise during the hymns, it's a good idea to choose well-known hymns to avoid embarrassed mumbling. This is especially important if you are not having a choir – too many weddings are remembered for the fact the vicar was the only one singing and this can be particularly noticeable when they are using a microphone! Popular hymns are 'Praise my soul the King of heaven', 'Lord of all hopefulness' and 'Love divine, all loves excelling'. Some ministers will not allow nationalistic hymns such as 'I vow to thee my country' or 'Jerusalem' so do double-check your choices. There is no equivalent of hymns for civil ceremonies and guests don't sing at any point.

Signing the Register

This is a good point for a long piece of music, or even two as signing the register can take a little time. Ideally, you need at least ten minutes of music and it's a wise idea to have a 'reserve' piece in case photographs here take longer than expected. Again, you can choose whatever you like but if you're having a civil ceremony, you need to make sure that there is no religious content in any of your choices.

The Recessional

If you want to really 'go for it' with your music, this is the moment as you make your exit as newlyweds. Don't hold back with the music here, make it as happy and as uplifting as possible! Classical choices include 'Canon in D' by Pachebel, Mendelssohn's 'Wedding March' or anything that's suitably celebratory. Modern choices are endless but U2's 'Beautiful Day' or even 'We Go Together' from Grease would certainly get the party going. It's often at this moment that some couples, particularly those having a civil ceremony, opt for a bit of humour and it's a great signal to guests that the more relaxed part of the day is now starting.

Readings

Readings are, if anything, a better way to make your ceremony your own. Unlike music, the reader and reading will have the absolute attention of the guests – there's no-one entering or exiting at the same time – and this is quite often an emotional moment. Obviously, who you choose to do your readings is up to you but you need someone with a good, clear voice who won't be unnerved by the prospect of reading in front of your other guests.

As with music, readings given at a civil ceremony are not allowed to contain any religious references, while it is customary to have at least one bible reading during a church service. Your registrar or minister will be able to give you some suggestions and wedding magazines often include little booklets of readings. There are also lots of places on the internet to search through but always have your readings approved by whoever will be taking the ceremony.

TAMRYN'S TIP

Give your readers plenty of opportunity to practise their readings ahead of the day and if you want their words to be a real tribute to you both, consider allowing them to choose their own piece, one which they feel best sums you up as a couple and one that they're happiest reading.

If you're asking someone to be a reader at your ceremony, a nice way to do it is to give them a gift-wrapped book of wedding readings (*Wedding Readings & Musical Ideas* by Rev. John Wynburne and Alison Gibbs, also published by Foulsham, for example – see 'Further Information' on page 253 for details). Attach a tag either asking them to choose one or give them the page reference of the piece you would like them to read for you. It's a very low-cost idea but one that will make them feel very special.

Ideally, readings should be:

* Of a reasonable length. Be wary about choosing anything that's too long – it's unfair on the reader and it's likely that your guests' attention levels may start to dip.
* Relevant to the bride and groom. A passage from a favourite book is a nice touch.
* Accessible. Your guests need to understand the text to make it meaningful. You might have read English Literature at Cambridge but don't assume all your guests will understand elaborate metaphors.

* Different. If you're having two readings, choose pieces with different themes or messages.
* Researched. There are hundreds of potential readings out there so don't simply plump for one that is popular. Take time to hunt for something that expresses everything you want to say.

Practice Makes Perfect?

For the majority of religious ceremonies, the wedding rehearsal is an integral part of the build-up to the day. Most take place in the week before the wedding day and it's a great opportunity to run through everything – who'll stand where, who will sit where, when the readings will take place, where you need to go to sign the register and generally what the main wedding party needs to be doing at every moment. Your officiant will be able to give you lots of advice and assistance, all of which will help to make the ceremony run very smoothly.

However, you do not have a rehearsal for a civil ceremony, which can be a bit daunting for some couples. The registrar will speak to those involved in the proceedings before the start of the ceremony to explain when they'll be called upon. Remember, however, that you will be led through your vows, so just listen carefully to the registrar and to any directions that they give you. To make things easier for everyone, it can be useful to think carefully about the ceremony before the day, using these questions to help you:

* Do you want your guests to sit on the traditional 'sides'? (The bride's friends and family sit on the left and the groom's guests on the right as you stand at the back of the room looking forward.)
* Do you want to reserve seats for anyone? Close family (parents or grandparents) along with the best man and bridesmaids are usually seated in the front two rows.

Remember that if the bridesmaids enter after everyone else, spaces need to be kept for them.

* Will the bridesmaids walk in before or after the bride? Walking in before has advantages, especially in smaller venues, as the bridesmaids can make their way to their seats easily without having to climb over the back of the bride's gown and their arrival gives the guests time to stand and prepare themselves for the bride.
* Where will your readers and witnesses sit? Ideally, they need to be in spots where they can get out easily when they are required to come forward.
* Who will play your music if you are having a CD? Will they be able to see when you are ready to make your entrance?
* After the ceremony, who will walk out with whom? If you want to be traditional, the best man should walk out with the chief bridesmaid followed by the groom's father with the bride's mother and vice versa.
* Who will look after your marriage certificate? Traditionally, it is given to the bride, which isn't very practical as bridal gowns don't come with pockets! Pick someone very trustworthy to look after this document for you.
* The mother of the bride usually arrives with the bridesmaids and then makes her way to her seat. It's nice for her to be escorted so perhaps delegate a close relative to this task if you are having a civil ceremony or an usher at a religious ceremony.

By working your way through the ceremony itself, you can plan ahead. Speak to your ushers or delegated person and give them clear instructions as to what needs to be done. Let them know if any guests will need assistance (for example, elderly relatives or friends with young children) and remind them to ask people to turn their mobile phones off on entering the ceremony room.

TAMRYN'S TIP

If you're having two ushers or helpers, try to pick one from each side of the family as it makes things a lot easier later on when they're helping to round people up for the photos!

CHAPTER CHECKLIST

So, that's the most important information on 'the main event' covered. I can't stress enough that for absolute clarification on exactly what is and isn't allowed, you need to speak with your officiant – regardless of what you may have read is allowed or was allowed at other weddings – as you need to be totally sure it will be permitted at yours. Ask questions and certainly confirm things before you print any orders of ceremony! Also remember:

* There are legal restrictions on when and where a ceremony can take place so find out the facts before you start planning.

* Ensure that you have all the necessary paperwork to begin the marriage process. Hunt out birth certificates and double-check what else you'll need to provide (proof of address, baptism certificates, etc.).

* Choose long enough pieces of music to cover the signing of the register and, if possible, have a 'reserve' piece if needed.

* Civil ceremony readings and music must not contain any religious references so anything containing the words 'heaven', 'spirit' or similar won't be allowed.

* Spend some time choosing your readings. This won't cost you a penny but will add to the occasion enormously.

* You won't get a rehearsal if you're having a civil ceremony. To avoid confusion, think through everything beforehand and make sure that your ushers are well briefed.

Five
The Venue

Deciding on the venue for your wedding – be it a venue suitable for both the ceremony and reception or one purely for the post-ceremony celebrations, is one of the first big 'fun' parts of wedding planning. Once you've chosen your venue, you can start thinking about menus, drinks, room layouts and decorations and begin to contact other suppliers who operate in that area. Of course, this all means you can start to tell people more about your day!

However, this is another of the biggest decisions you'll make about your wedding day so to help make it your ideal day, you need to be organised and systematic. When you begin to research and visit venues, it's incredibly easy to be overwhelmed by a gorgeous-looking building with fabulous grounds and start to picture yourself, your partner, and all your guests enjoying the day there. This is totally understandable because you want a venue where you feel at home – there's no point booking somewhere that makes you feel on edge or uneasy in any way but you must try to think rationally. This is in order to ask the right questions and to ensure that you're armed with all the information that will allow you to make the right decision. As stunning as venues can look, you need to be sure that the staff understand you and your hopes and plans for the day, that the venue charges are within budget and that you're not going to be hit with any unwelcome surprises further down the line. If I could give you just one tip related to venue hunting, it would be to ask as many questions as you want because only then can you both be sure that you've chosen the perfect venue.

The Cost of a Great Venue

After spending time working on your budget, you'll be aware that the venue and its related costs make up a massive proportion of your total wedding spend, so before you agree to hand over such a huge sum of money, you need to be sure that you've accounted for everything. Venue charges are rarely just as simple as room hire and catering. There are often lots of little additional charges that can pop up and nibble into your budget contingency if you've not checked on them earlier. When you start to research venues, noting all of the costs involved is one of the first things that you should do. There is little point in falling in love with a venue if it's not within your budget. Some of the charges that you need to be looking out for are as follows.

Ceremony Fees

If you're hoping to hold your civil ceremony at an approved venue, you will be charged for this. This fee is unavoidable and is often a few hundred pounds, but as this cost is determined by the venue themselves and not by the registrars, it can vary.

Room Hire

You may be charged room hire fees for your reception. Some venues will waive this charge if you're having your ceremony at the venue or if you're catering for over a certain amount of people so it's best to check. Room hire charges can vary immensely but will often be around £250. You may get something in return such as a free room for the bride and groom if the venue also provides accommodation.

Exclusive Use

Costs for exclusive use run into the thousands and may or may not include other services, so double-check exactly what you get for your money before making a booking.

Late Licence

If you don't want your party to end at 11pm, you can ask your venue if they will apply for a late licence on your behalf. You need to request this in writing and there's often a charge, usually in the region of £50.

Food and Drink

This is likely to be the biggest cost from the venue! After your final meeting when you provide the venue with numbers of guests and meals, they'll prepare your final invoice based on these numbers. If anyone drops out after this point, it's very unlikely that you'll get a refund. This invoice will probably have to be paid before the date and you should check it thoroughly to make sure that you're paying for exactly what you've booked. You should be able to get an idea of food and drink costs from a venue's information pack by adding up the cost of a meal, drinks and evening buffet and simply multiplying that by the number of guests you hope to invite.

Damage Waivers

Most venues have rules about damage, whether it's a rip in the carpet or a pin hole made in the wall and cover themselves by charging a damage waiver. If, after your wedding nothing has been marked, you'll probably get this back but if there's been a problem, the cost of repairs will be taken from this amount. Depending on the type of venue, this charge can be about a hundred pounds or much more for an historic building.

Hire Costs

Venues that are an empty canvas such as a hall, school or museum can be great as you can literally turn them into anything that you like. However, you will probably have to bear the brunt of the costs involved in hiring tables, chairs, bar equipment and other catering essentials. This might be arranged through your caterer or via the venue itself but be aware that fees that initially look appealing and very competitive can dramatically increase when you have to add in items that may well be included in fees from other venues.

Miscellaneous Costs

These are quite often the costs that you're faced with close to the day that you weren't expecting and so they're most likely to be the ones that can leave you with a slightly sour taste in your mouth. Will you be charged for bringing in your own DJ as opposed to using the venue's preferred supplier? Will you be faced with an additional charge if you would like your venue to cut and serve your wedding cake? If you want to deliver items to the site the day before the event, will the venue add on a storage fee? Think clearly about what you want and ask the venue if they can assist with your request, in writing, if you want total clarification. It's easy to assume that things will be included but it's wise not to.

Paying

So, once you've got a fair idea of the costs involved, you'll need to know that you can afford it and then how you are going to pay for it. Venue charges are usually made in stages so you won't return home to one gigantic bill! The majority of venues make one charge as a deposit when you book (usually in the region of £500, depending on the venue), with another charge at a pre-determined point. The balance is then due a week or two before your wedding date, after you've provided final numbers for food and drink (if the venue is providing that for you). However, all venues are different. Some allow you to pay on the day itself and others will invoice you afterwards for costs, so again, be sure you know exactly when your payments will be due before you commit to your favoured venue.

Various Types of Venue

The range of locations that now market themselves as wedding venues is immense so there's somewhere for every style and every budget. Whether you're after rural charm or urban chic, brand new or incredibly old, there will be the place out there for you. So, here's a little rundown of the variety of venues on offer, as well as a rough guide to prices.

Hotels

Hotels are a very popular choice for many couples. They're often beautifully furnished, well sized and have all the things on-site for you such as kitchens, accommodation and most importantly lots of space. One criticism of hotels, especially the larger chains or groups, is their tendency to only do 'packages' so you pay a certain amount for everything which doesn't leave you much option to make things personal or bring in your own suppliers. However, this isn't true of everywhere so if there's a gorgeous hotel you've got your eye on, get some information and check it out. If you're just booking a few rooms and catering, costs are relatively low (depending on the style of the hotel). Smaller country house hotels often offer 'exclusive use' which is great as you can take over the building for the day/night and not have other guests wandering around but this can add to the costs involved.
Price range – low to high

Stately Homes/Castles

This is the option for the seriously glam wedding! Lots of stately homes and castles are now promoting themselves as wedding venues and if you want a guaranteed 'wow' factor, this could be the thing to go for. They can be more expensive than hotels but are often a little more personal which can be a great plus point if you want something a bit different. As most are open to the public, summer weddings are often limited to certain days of the week or there are restrictions as to which rooms you are able to use. Most will offer sole usage but this often comes at quite a price. Heritage buildings usually insist that you use suppliers from their pre-approved list but that's not always the case and you can be restricted with decorations (for example, no candles or confetti).

Price range – medium to high

Conference Centres

Not all conference centres are built like office blocks. Some are housed in very attractive buildings with spacious grounds and other facilities, such as swimming pools or games areas, which can be great if you're hoping guests will stay for a night or two. You can be sure that the people who work there are very used to organising big functions and meetings and therefore equipment levels are usually very good. Rates here can often be very reasonable at weekends as the majority of the centre's business takes place during the working week so you're not taking over rooms at their peak times and most will offer well-priced accommodation too. Rooms can be a little functional but some carefully though-out decoration can easily rectify this.

Price range – low to medium

Marquees

These are always popular for weddings and give you a great deal of flexibility over your arrangements. They can be designed to fit any space, to provide any amount of facilities and for any number of guests. Some marquees are permanent fixtures in the grounds of venues and some are specially erected for a function. If you've got large gardens at a house available to you or you can use grounds at a sports club, school or farm, a marquee would suit you perfectly. A good marquee company can design a structure to suit your budget but you must be aware of health and safety concerns for wires, provision of electricity supplies and fire extinguishers. You'll also need to think about running water for caterers and toilet facilities for guests. A marquee is a great blank canvas that can be transformed into anything you like but you will probably need to add in furniture and equipment hire to the basic cost in many cases.

Price range – medium to high

'Other Use' Venues

An increasing number of venues can be used for wedding receptions that have other functions. Schools, society/ association headquarters or private clubs, for example, can provide excellent space for weddings. It can be a wonderful trip down memory lane to return to your past school for your reception and prices are usually very reasonable. Clubs or headquarters are often better equipped than schools and many are interesting buildings in themselves.

Price range – low to medium

Restaurants

In many ways, these are perfect wedding venues because you're almost guaranteed good food and drink! They are often well suited to smaller wedding parties because of their more intimate feel and often have lots of private dining areas so you won't be with other diners. You won't need to hire in any equipment but sometimes space outside for photographs can be limited as can areas for dancing.

Price range – medium

Council-funded Buildings

I know that the phrase 'council-funded building' probably doesn't conjure up images of venues that would feel particularly suitable for a wedding, but I promise that you will be surprised. A lot of civic buildings are housed in beautifully designed spaces and, as they are partly funded by the council, prices are a lot lower than you would expect. If you're looking for a city centre venue at a good price, considering a council building is a great idea.

Price range – low to medium

Halls

Village, town or sports halls are great options for wedding venues if you're not planning to spend huge amounts of your allotted funds on your wedding venue. They're spacious and very flexible, as once you've paid the hall-hire fee, you really can decide how much you want to spend. If you want to use their chairs and tables, that's great, or if you want to hire items in, that's great too. You can choose a caterer that will work to any budget you like, your decorations can be simple or more extravagant and you can use the space available exactly how you want with no choruses of 'this is how we usually do things' from venue staff. The downside is that you're unlikely to have any dedicated on-site staff to help you set things up on the day itself or to assist you in the run-up to the wedding.

Price range – low

Unusual

Whatever you're into or if you just fancy something completely different for your wedding venue, there will be somewhere for you. Everywhere from zoos, museums, ships, piers, steam trains, arboretums to theatres can be available for hire as your venue. If you really want something different and memorable, this could be an avenue that's worth going down. You'd probably have to arrange your own caterers and equipment hire and there might be some stricter rules and regulations, but if you can live with those things, you're guaranteed a very unique day.

Price range – medium to high

Doing Your Homework

Starting to research venues is one of the really enjoyable parts of wedding planning. For most couples, it's also the first tangible thing they do towards the day after the essential (but not very enthralling) tasks of budgeting and organising. There are quite a few ways to start your research.

Phone Directory

Your local area phone directory is a great place to start and classified directories such as the Yellow Pages (www.yell.com) have huge sections dedicated to wedding venues. Also check out the hotels and conference centres section if you're looking for somewhere simply for a reception.

Wedding Websites

A check through any of the major wedding websites (there are details of the most popular at the back of this book) is also a great idea. Most have venue directories where you can search by area or venue type and many come with reviews from brides who have held their weddings at the locations listed.

Registry Office

Most can provide you with a list of approved venues that fall within their jurisdiction if you ask them. Office details can be found in your phonebook or on a website such as www.yell.com if you're looking at a venue further afield.

Magazines

Lots of venues advertise in wedding magazines and there are indeed some that are completely dedicated to sites suitable for receptions or ceremonies. The 'real weddings' section can also be a good place to look for inspiration.

Web Search

Enter 'Wedding Venue' and your preferred county or area into any of the major search engines and you'll be rewarded with a long list of possibilities.

Friends and Family

Does anyone know of any fantastic hotels or venues? Have they heard great things about a particular venue recently? Ask around and you never know what you might find out.

Which One?

So, now you've got a long list of venues in the area that you want. The next step is to start gathering some information on each of them so you can begin to narrow down your selection. Either call or e-mail each venue to provisionally check their availability on your date and to request their wedding information pack (some venue websites have their brochures available for download directly which is fabulous for saving time). I have to admit that my supplier selection starts well before I even receive a brochure or pack as I mentally mark down venues or companies that don't reply promptly and courteously, make errors with my address or name or don't actually send me what I've asked for. It doesn't take long to reply to an e-mail or to put information in an envelope and you want a venue that is interested enough in you to get back to you as quickly as possible when you request something. Once all the relevant packs have been posted or e-mailed to you, you can start wading through them and noting the following:

* **Costs:** Are the costs within your budget? If not, there's really no point in going any further with that venue, however gorgeous it looks. Breaking your budget so early on in the planning will have huge knock-on effects for funds you've allocated to other suppliers. Be strict with yourselves.

THE VENUE

* **Size:** Can they accommodate wedding parties of the size that you're planning on inviting?
* **Location:** Is the location convenient for you? Does it have areas for photographs?
* **Catering:** Do you like the look of the sample menus and drinks lists?
* **Suppliers:** Are you allowed free reign over your suppliers or do you have to choose from the venue's approved lists?
* **Other weddings:** Will other wedding parties be there on the same day or do they only hold one per day?
* **Flexibility:** How flexible are they? Do you have to make your choices from a set number of packages or can you put things together to suit yourselves?
* **Payments:** When are you required to pay balances? How much is the deposit?
* **Notes:** Is there anything of interest noted in the 'small print' such as restrictions on decoration or minimum required numbers that must be catered for?
* **Overall:** What is your overall impression of the venue from the information that you've received? Is it well put together? What are your gut feelings? Does the look of the venue match the style of wedding you're hoping for?

There are no 'right and wrong' answers to the above questions. The venue is a purely personal choice and what you're looking for will be different to other couples, so take your time. It's quite useful to try to rank the venues in order of preference at this stage because, however many are still in the running, it's a good idea to try and limit the number that you actually visit. There's no denying that venue visits take up quite a bit of time, especially when you factor in travelling, and the more you see, the more confusing it can become. Try and organise visits to your top four in one weekend and go from there. It's always best to make an appointment to visit so that you can be sure an appropriate member of staff will be available to show you around and answer your questions. Once you've done your research, you're ready to start visiting and make a choice.

Visiting Venues

On your first visit to a venue, remember that first impressions count so what does the place look like as you drive up to it? Does it look well maintained and is there plenty of parking space? Another thing to look at is obviously the staff. These are quite likely to be the people who'll be looking after you and your guests, so do you want happy and efficient or bored and uninterested staff? On your visit, you should get a full tour of the venue, including a look at the ceremony room (if applicable), dining room, bars, function rooms and bedrooms. It's also a good idea to have a look around the grounds to see how photogenic things are.

TAMRYN'S TIP

Try and go about the same time in the year as the date of your wedding so you can get an idea of what things will look like on your big day. Take a look at the gardens, the light (for photographs) and make sure there's shade and seating if you're hoping to get outside.

The person who shows you around should be able to answer your questions and you should try and find out the following:

* How many people can they accommodate in the various rooms?

* Do they offer full meals or various buffets? Can they cater for barbecues or hog roasts?
* Are they planning any price increases to food, drink and other items between your visit and your wedding date?
* Are there any planned room refurbishments or building works?
* Do you have to use their drink or can you provide your own? If you can, how much is their corkage charge?
* How do they cater for vegetarians or people with other dietary requirements?
* Do they allow confetti/rice/bubbles?
* Are you allowed to use candles?
* Do they provide a stand for the cake/table plan or any other table stationery such as menus or place cards?
* Do they use linen or paper napkins/table covers?
* How many different ways can they lay the tables out in the room?
* What's the venue's policy on smoking?
* When can suppliers get in to the venue to set up in the morning?
* When does everything have to be cleared by?
* Can you get a late licence for the bar? Is there a charge for this?
* How many waiting/bar staff will be allocated to you on the day?
* Check the parking/toilet facilities.
* Find out exactly when they need final numbers and what their policy is on alterations to details after that point.
* Do they have someone who can act as toastmaster if required?
* If you pay for a certain amount of alcohol, what happens if it's not all used? Also, what would happen if what you've paid for runs out?

* What are their booking terms with regards to deposits and balances?
* Can you block-book accommodation and do they give any form of discount to guests?
* Can you taste-test the food or wine before you make a final decision? Is there a charge for this?
* If you're planning a summer wedding with drinks outside etc., find out what would happen in the event of bad weather.
* If you're having a band or DJ, is there somewhere they can change?
* Is there somewhere secure where you can store wedding gifts?
* Do they allow guests to start a tab for drinks or does everything have to be paid for in cash?

Making Your Decision

The list of questions that you could ask is literally endless but just make sure you find out about the things that are most important to you, not what the venue wants to tell you! Only you know whether being able to dance until dawn is the crucial factor in deciding on your venue so use the priority lists that you will have drawn up during your brainstorming sessions to make sure that your selected site meets all your criteria.

If you're feeling positive about a venue, make sure that they still have availability for your date before you leave. Are they able to 'pencil you in' for a few weeks to give you time to make your decision? Ask about the booking procedure before you depart as well – how much are you required to pay as a deposit? If you're then heading off to visit another venue, make a few quick notes before you arrive at the next location because it's quite easy for things to become a little blurred once you've seen a few rooms and gardens!

Once you've visited your shortlisted venues, it's quite likely that you'll have a pretty clear idea which one it will be that you book. If not, think about the 'pros and cons' of each site or even book a second visit and take someone else for a second opinion. Whilst you're making your decision, do keep in contact with the venue because it isn't unknown for someone else to book up in the interim period. Ask that they keep you informed if anyone else shows an interest in your date so that you're not disappointed.

When you've made your decision, let the venue know as soon as possible. Some might require you to put your confirmation in writing before they send out contracts and others will be happy with a verbal 'yes' over the phone.

TAMRYN'S TIP

If other venues have your date on hold, do let them know when you've made a decision so that they can release that date to other couples. If you feel uncomfortable about doing this, an e-mail or voicemail message is fine!

Contacts and Contracts

After you've told your chosen venue that you'd like to go ahead and book, they will send you a confirmation form or contract. At this point, this will confirm the main details of the day and will include your names, address(es), date of wedding, room or rooms that you will be using, other services they will be providing such as food and drink and any other relevant information. There's unlikely to be a mention of the final bill at this point (although they may include an estimate) and any costs that are listed will be noted as being subject to change. You need to double-check that all the information that they have about you is correct and note when you need to provide them with final numbers and choices for your food and drink as this can affect when you can send out your invitations (this is discussed further in Chapter 9). Any information regarding dates for further deposits should also be put into your planning file and budget spreadsheet. Before you sign and return the contract to them, read all the terms and conditions thoroughly to make sure there's no hidden surprises and nothing that contradicts what you were told at your visits. If you want to question anything or if you just want clarification on any point, ask now because once you've signed and returned the contract, it's too late.

Make a copy of the contract for yourself before you post it back to the venue so you can refer to it during your planning if necessary. When you return the contract to them, request that they acknowledge your booking and deposit payment in writing. The majority of venues will do this anyway, but you need to be sure that they've received everything.

Congratulations, you've just booked your wedding venue!

Interim Visits

If you're booking your venue some way in advance, it's quite likely that you'll want to visit before the day, perhaps to show family members or suppliers around. Interim visits aren't a problem for most venues but it's always a good idea to call and check that you can gain access to the rooms that you want to see. It's probable that other functions will be booked for a majority of weekends, while for some venues staff will need to know you're coming to unlock buildings or to pass on parking permits to you.

If you ask any questions of your venue after booking, do try to get their answers in writing (this is where e-mail is extremely helpful!). Similarly, don't assume that your venue will be able to do something, check. It might seem reasonable to you that you can cut your cake after the main course and have it served a few minutes later with coffee but you need to check before you firm up your plans.

TAMRYN'S TIP

It can be a great idea to take some photographs of your venue on one of these trips. You can use these images to jog your memory of the rooms between visits when you're planning decorations or to show them to suppliers if necessary.

You should also confirm who your contact will be both in the build-up to your wedding day and on the day itself. It's not uncommon for venue-based wedding co-ordinators to not actually work at weekends! They hand over to banqueting or function managers on the day which means that you won't be working with the person who's been with you during your planning. If this is the case, make sure that you meet the member of staff who will be in charge of your wedding beforehand so that they're familiar with you and your plans. Alternatively, book an independent wedding co-ordinator who can oversee the wedding day itself and work in your best interests at all times. This can help provide you with continuity throughout your planning and make sure that, come the big day, there's a single point of contact for all suppliers.

Final Meetings

A month or so before your big day, you should have a final meeting with the reception venue to run through everything you've organised and to ensure that they're fully aware of all of the timings and plans for the day. From this meeting, the venue will produce their notes that they will use on the day itself. Make sure you get a copy of these. That way you can double-check they understand everything that you've arranged. At your final meeting, you'll need to tell your venue:

* Final numbers of guests for the dinner/evening reception.
* Numbers requiring meals and a breakdown of the number of meat and vegetarian meals.
* Numbers of children's meals that will be required and any highchairs that need to be provided.
* Details of food and drink that are to be provided for suppliers and where you want them to eat.
* How you want the tables to be set out and how many settings are to be on each table.
* Where you want the cake table and stand.
* The time that your florist, cake maker and other suppliers will arrive.
* How you want the cake cut and which tiers to save.
* Timings for the meal and evening reception.
* Who they should speak to on the day if they have any questions (for example, father of the bride, best man or your independent wedding co-ordinator).
* If the venue also provides accommodation you'll need to confirm the names of people wanting rooms (also tell them if anyone wants an early check-in).
* Whether you wish to have a receiving line, when the speeches will be and who will be speaking.
* Some suppliers, especially musicians, need car parking spaces to be reserved for them so be sure to tell your venue if this facility is needed.
* Do you want any floral arrangements or other decorations to be given to guests at the end?
* What you would like done with items remaining on the tables after everyone has left.
* What announcements, if any, you would like them to make for you, e.g. announcing you into dinner?
* Whether you want your napkins rolled or folded. (This may sound like a little thing but I've had to unfold and roll 100 napkins that the hotel had folded without

checking. As the bride had made napkin rings, she didn't want them folded!).

By this point, you will know your wedding plans in great detail so talk through everything. If you are particularly worried about any part of the day or if any guests need some extra attention, let people know. The more you tell everyone who is working on your day, the more likely it is that they can get everything absolutely perfect for you.

CHAPTER CHECKLIST

This chapter should have helped you to make one of the biggest decisions about your wedding day as well as providing you with information that you'll need throughout your dealings with your venue. The most important things are:

* Get answers to any of your questions in writing if possible.

* Make sure you know when all the venue payments are due.

* Meet whoever will be in charge of your wedding day.

* Tell your venue as much as possible about your plans at your final meeting – you know everything inside out but don't assume everyone else does!

* Allocate someone to be the venue's point of contact on the day, be it your best man or independent wedding co-ordinator, and make sure they're fully briefed so they can handle everything for you.

* If you want clarification on anything your venue is telling you, keep asking until you get it.

Six
The Reception

The word 'wedding reception' used to mean an evening buffet and a slightly dodgy DJ but now it has so many more connotations. There are many more options open to the bridal couple these days, which is great because you can choose whatever suits you best but it is this choice that can make things tougher too. How do you know what to do? Can you be sure that your plans will work? Well, this chapter should certainly help you.

Drinks and Dinner Reception

This is probably the most common form of reception. Usually guests are invited for celebratory drinks following the ceremony and then onto dinner, in whatever format you've chosen. Obviously, if you're having a religious ceremony, guests will have to make their way to your reception venue before the party can start whereas couples who've had a civil wedding literally just need to walk out of the ceremony room to start their reception! This type of reception gives you time to mingle with your guests and have photographs taken before everyone makes their way in to dinner.

Compared to the levels of organisation that often go in to other parts of the day, the drinks and dinner reception can seem relatively easy. Serve drinks and a little while later, serve dinner? Sounds simple enough, doesn't it? Well, it can be because this part of the day is usually in the hands of your venue's banqueting staff or your caterer. However, there are plenty of things you can do to make sure that the atmosphere is absolutely amazing:

* Don't let the drinks reception go on too long! It's very tempting to prolong this part of the day but 1–2 hours is certainly enough time. After a while, standing around starts to lose its appeal and your guests will begin to flag. Keep this section of the day short and if you want to, build in more 'free time' after dinner before any dancing starts. You'll have plenty of time to chat to everyone then and your guests will be more relaxed after they've had something to eat and a chance to sit down.
* If you're limiting the numbers of celebratory drinks you provide, make sure the bar is open so that guests can get themselves more drinks if they want to. If it's a hot day or if guests have been travelling in the morning, you don't want anyone getting dehydrated.
* Do make sure there are some spots for guests to sit down. This is particularly important if you are inviting elderly guests, but standing for a couple of hours is a lot to expect of most people.
* Try to keep everyone in one area. I don't mean that you need to pen them in like sheep but it's much easier (and quicker!) if the majority of people are in one space when you're trying to get everyone together for photographs. And the faster you can get the group shots done, the more time you will have to spend with people.
* Allow some time for everyone to take their seats for dinner. This can often take longer than you think because the moment dinner is announced, guests suddenly decide to go to the toilet, get one last drink from the bar or come and have a chat with you. My tip here is for you both to sneak off for a few minutes'

peace just before dinner is announced as this will stop people hanging around to talk to you and guarantees you both a little bit of time on your own.

Evening Receptions

The 'evening reception' is basically the party that most couples really look forward to! After the more formal aspects of the day, it's a chance for everyone to relax and really enjoy themselves. Many couples invite additional guests to the evening reception (usually work colleagues or friends of their parents) and this is a great opportunity to have fun with your nearest and dearest. I always find that the atmosphere during the evening is completely different to that during the day – couples who were very nervous realise that they've made it through the more stressful parts of the day and can now really enjoy themselves and even the most 'traditional' weddings change completely once the music starts! We will talk about entertainment options in Chapter 11 but of course there are other things to bear in mind:

* Give evening guests a big welcome. It's all too easy for evening guests to slip un-noticed into the venue which isn't a very nice feeling for them, particularly if they've travelled far to be part of the event. Make sure someone is there to welcome them whether it's you, the best man, a bridesmaid or your parents. Tell them where they can leave their coats, point them in the direction of the bar, let them know when the first dance will be and generally show them how pleased you are that they are there.

* Make sure everyone knows when the first dance is going to be. As much as some couples wish no-one was there to witness this, guests love to watch the first dance so give them all the chance to see it. And if you really don't want to dance on your own for an entire

song, ask the DJ or band to invite people onto the dance floor after the first chorus.

✳ If you're serving food or cake in the evening, make sure everyone knows where to find it! There's nothing worse than spending money on food and having huge amounts left over because no-one knew where it was. Ask the best man or the ushers to let your guests know when and where they can find some nibbles.

✳ Don't stay until the very end of the evening. Of course, most couples want to enjoy every minute of their party but even if you're staying overnight at the venue, it's still nice to make an exit. Have a last dance and a big send-off – this way you leave with your last memory being a packed dance floor and lots of happy smiling faces. Staying until the bitter end means that you'll see all the mess and party leftovers which isn't so nice!

Doing it Differently

Of course, there's absolutely no wedding laws that state your wedding has to run like this and there are other options open to you if you fancy breaking the mould a little. If you decide to shake things up, do be as clear as possible in your invitations and other information as to exactly what you're planning. Guests aren't psychic and they won't know what the format of the day is going to be unless you tell them. Obviously, you might want to keep some things a secret until the day but letting them know times, locations and what will be provided in the way of food will make them much happier!

Here are some ideas to get you thinking.

Afternoon Only

You don't have to party late if you don't want to. A nice alternative is the 'afternoon only' reception. This is great if you want to invite lots of people to your ceremony but would prefer a more intimate family dinner in the evening. After the ceremony, guests can have drinks and canapés (or even afternoon tea) and there's time for photographs, cake cutting and even the speeches before the majority leave and close friends and family head to a private dinner. Three or four hours is a good length of time here so this would work well with an earlier ceremony. Because you're not having to provide a larger meal for so many guests, it's a great way to have a big wedding on a smaller budget.

Pre-ceremony Drinks

If you're having a later ceremony, having drinks (and nibbles if you're providing them) before the ceremony can work really well. This has benefits in that it guarantees that all guests will arrive in plenty of time for the ceremony, the groom and families get time to mingle with guests, there's time for some photos and everyone gets to know each other before the ceremony. Then you can limit the time after the ceremony for the remaining photos before moving on to dinner or an evening reception if you prefer.

Big Evening Buffet

Perhaps you'd prefer to provide the majority of the food in the evening (and, being realistic, how often do you really fancy a three-course meal at 4.30pm?!). So you might choose to provide canapés or an afternoon tea immediately after the ceremony and then something like a hog roast in the evening when people are naturally more hungry.

Don't be scared to 'do things differently' – just think things through properly. When will guests arrive? When will they leave? When will you be able to build in time for photographs, mingling, entertainment and food? Don't feel that you 'have' to provide certain amounts of food and drink at your wedding to entice guests to come. People will want to be there to share the day with you and their attendance shouldn't be based on how often they'll be fed and watered. Have the celebration

THE RECEPTION

that you want and be clear to people what you're doing. You'll be more relaxed on the day when it's what you want and that will transfer to your guests. Having a wedding that you're not really comfortable with will be evident to all.

The Formalities

Whatever format you decide to go for, there are 'formalities' that you'll need to think about, even if you eventually choose to omit them from the day. Of course, you can easily juggle elements around in your plan of the day if that suits you best. To help you pull that off I've included details on all the things that you'll need to consider because making changes always has knock-on effects for other areas of your plan.

Receiving Line

This is traditionally the moment when all your guests are introduced to the parents of the bride and the parents of the groom before getting a few words with the bride and groom themselves. It most often takes place as guests are making their way into dinner but can also be done on arrival at your reception venue.

TAMRYN'S TIP

When you're greeting guests, try to stay with your new husband or wife. It's all too easy to split up and when you look back on the day, you have very few shared memories. Stick together, introduce each other to guests and then move on – and it's easier to do that when you're together as well.

An advantage of having a traditional receiving line is that all the guests get to speak with the main members of the wedding party but it can take a long time! For 100 guests, you need to allow around half an hour, so if you're not going to have much time before dinner, a receiving line can really eat into this section of the day. An alternative would be to have only the bride and groom in the line on entry to dinner or have the parents greeting guests more informally as they arrive, all of which can cut down on the amount of time you'll need. Alternatively, you can ditch the receiving line altogether. But if you decide to do this, you really need to make an effort to speak to as many guests as possible.

Speeches

Usually, the speeches take place at the end of the meal but more couples are choosing to have them before dinner. This is great if the speakers are nervous and want to get their speech out of the way so that they can relax and enjoy dinner. However, if you want to do this, you need to be quite strict with those speaking about the amount of time that they have for their speech. Remember that the kitchen staff or your caterers will be working to a very precise schedule to ensure your food is ready at exactly the right moment so speeches that run on past the allotted time risk ruining their hard work. Also, since at this point guests might be a little peckish, make sure that there's bread and butter on the tables when guests enter so they can nibble if necessary during the speeches.

You'll also need to consider toast drinks – during a 'traditional' day, the toast drinks are poured after the dessert plates are cleared from the tables and the coffee has been served. If you want to have the speeches before the meal, you'll need to decide whether the glasses will be on the tables ready as guests enter or whether staff will pour after everyone has sat down. Pouring the champagne after everyone has sat down can be quite time consuming and obviously the speeches can't start until everyone has a drink. It might be worth, therefore, asking if your venue can have the glasses ready filled 'behind the scenes' and then bring them out and serve them from trays once everyone has sat down. This takes a lot less time and still looks impressive.

Announcements

Even couples going for an informal-style of wedding usually have a few announcements made and everyone's favourite is when they're announced into dinner. For most couples, this is their first opportunity to be called 'Mr and Mrs' but some opt to be introduced as 'The bride and groom' or even simply by their first names. This is an absolutely brilliant moment as usually all the guests give you a really rousing welcome with lots of cheering and clapping as you take your seats. If you're not having a formal dinner, you might still like to be introduced to your guests at some point and make a big entrance. Look carefully at your plans to work out when will be the best moment – could you sneak off immediately after the ceremony and let your guests congregate for drinks before you make your big entrance? This might give you time for a few 'couple photographs' before you begin mingling.

Cake Cutting

Again, this is usually done after the meal but more and more people are choosing other times for this. If you're going to serve the cake with coffee after the meal, you'll need to have your cake-cutting moment almost as soon as you enter dinner so that the catering staff have plenty of time to cut it up. If you're not planning on serving it until later in the evening, there's no real rush to cut it up so some couples use the cutting as the official start to their evening reception and then take to the dance floor straight afterwards. You can also cut it after the speeches and use that as the 'end' of the formal part of the day. There are plenty of options open to you so think about when you're going to need the cake and work from there.

Timings

Working out the timings for your wedding day can always be quite tricky because it's so hard to know how long you need to allow for everything and how everything will run on the day. Obviously, the time of your ceremony is the most important element to consider as this will affect how you time the rest of the day. It can be a tough job because there's a very fine line between allowing too much time and feeling as though the day is stalling at various points and allowing too little time and feeling like the entire event has passed you by.

There's no real right and wrong answer but, as I mentioned earlier, don't let your drinks reception drag on too long – give yourself extra time in the evening instead when everyone will be more relaxed. Bear in mind especially that if you've invited additional guests for the evening, some might arrive early and there's nothing worse than having more people arriving when you've not finished your dessert! Here's some more information to help you decide on timings for the day:

* Think about the number of group photographs that you want to have taken and speak with your photographer to make sure there's enough time.
* If you're serving canapés between the ceremony and dinner, you can get away with allowing a little more time at that point.
* Speak with your venue or caterers about the meal or any food that you plan to serve – you'll probably need to allow around two hours for a three-course meal and then build in time for speeches as well.
* If the room that you're eating in will also become the room that the evening reception will be held in, all your guests will need to vacate the space so that it can be 'turned around' before the dancing starts. It usually takes around half an hour to clear tables, replace table cloths as necessary and to allow a band or DJ to set

THE RECEPTION

up. It might be worth considering serving coffee in a lounge or other area to encourage guests to move to speed this process up!

✳ Do find out how long any evening entertainment will take to set up – some bands or DJs with a lot of equipment need over half an hour so don't plan on having your first dance straight after dessert unless things have been set up before the meal.

Overall, however, there are only two things you really need to keep on time and they are the ceremony and the meal! After that, if your first dance is ten minutes late or if you have five fewer minutes of mingling than you'd planned, it's not the end of the world. Caterers will usually build in some contingency into their time plans for the meal but don't rely on this – aim to be on time for your meal. Your guests will thank you for it and, on the day itself, you'll probably be glad of the chance to sit down and take a bit of a breather as well.

What's Going On?

The trick with making the day as seamless as possible is to keep guests informed and almost to lead them through the event as much as possible. Your best man or a wedding day co-ordinator can be invaluable here – they should be liaising with the catering staff over timings for the meal, checking with photographers and videographers that they're going to be able to get all the shots and footage that they need and adjusting plans as required. Someone also needs to be on hand to answer any questions that guests have – making them feel looked after and pampered is a big step toward making the day excellent for them.

Elderly Guests

It can be a good idea to invite elderly guests to take their seats for dinner before the announcement is made to the rest of the guests. There's the possibility that it will take them longer to make their way into dinner, particularly if there are stairs at the venue, so allowing them to do this without other people rushing by them or making them feel that they're holding everyone up can be wise.

Guests with Children

Check if children will need highchairs. Let parents know where they can leave pushchairs and where they can go to change nappies if necessary. Some parents might need milk or other food heating up so ensure they know who to ask.

Guests with Special Dietary Requirements

Let guests know that their dietary requirements have been passed on to the venue or caterers but that they should ask the serving staff if they have any questions.

Keep in mind that you need to let guests know what is happening, even more so if you're doing things differently. You can do this by means of an information sheet, a personal wedding website, or you could have someone on hand on the day to be a point of contact for queries and who can help the day to flow by working with all the suppliers and making appropriate announcements and requests to guests. You may think that having a wedding day co-ordinator is an unnecessary expense but they can ensure that everything that you've planned (and paid for) happens at the right time and in the right way so their fee will guarantee that nothing is wasted. Having someone who you can rely on, be it a professional or a member of the wedding party, will also take a lot of stress off you both and allow you to enjoy your day. You shouldn't be having to direct guests to the bathrooms or be answering questions about your plans, you should just be left to enjoy every minute of the day.

CHAPTER CHECKLIST

This chapter has given you an overview of receptions, variations on the traditional format and information on things you need to keep in mind whilst you're planning. If you only take a few things from this chapter, let it be these:

❉ There are plenty of alternatives to the wedding norm of drinks, dinner and dancing if you'd prefer to do something different. Make sure that your plans are clearly communicated to guests so people aren't expecting things that won't be happening.

❉ Be wary about allowing more than an hour and half for a simple drinks reception before food is served. It's a long time for guests to be standing around and after a while, the fabulous atmosphere that you've built up will start to disappear as people get tired and hungry.

❉ It's easy to move activities around in the plan of the day to suit you as long as you think through the consequences of such alterations. Saying that you want speeches before the meal can have a knock-on effect so be sure you've thought clearly about other things that will need to be re-arranged as a result.

❉ Make sure that there is always someone on hand to look after your guests, to keep them informed of the plans, make any requests that are necessary and to liaise with all the suppliers. If the photographer needs an extra ten minutes to take a big group photo, someone needs to be there to communicate the change to the catering staff. The best weddings appear seamless to guests and even to the bride and groom. This takes work behind the scenes and someone needs to ensure that messages are being passed on and decisions are being made.

Seven
Food and Drink

The food served at a wedding is always one of the highlights of the day and the meal itself is a great opportunity for friends, family and, of course, the bride and groom to be able to relax after the formalities of the day and enjoy each other's company. Typically called a 'wedding breakfast', this tradition dates back hundreds of years to the feasts that took place after a wedding where eating together symbolised friendship and new allegiances.

Wedding breakfasts today are just as important and every couple wants to see all their loved ones having a great time over dinner. As such, arrangements surrounding the meal are often some of the most complicated and carefully considered of the day. What do you need to serve? Who sits next to whom? Can you do anything differently and most importantly, how can you put your own stamp on the proceedings at this point?

Your Catering Budget

Obviously before you start finalising your menus, you'll need to look carefully at your budget. Your venue should provide you with a menu pack and you will probably have a good idea of the numbers of guests that you hope to invite so you should be able to start calculating the cost of the various food and drink options that are open to you. It can also be helpful to think back to your brainstorming and budget setting – did you mark catering as being one of your priorities? Are you food lovers who are happy to cut back in other areas to provide fantastic food or are you not really bothered by fancy menus and vintage champagne? As with all things, the only right answer is the one that suits you both. Providing food and drink for your guests is the biggest cost involved in any wedding of any budget so be prepared for this to take a real chunk out of the money you've set aside for the day.

TAMRYN'S TIP

When you're looking at guest numbers and food and drink prices, don't rely on anyone not accepting your invitation to bring the cost within your budget. Make sure you can afford to cater for everyone you hope to invite and if a few people do decline, use the spare funds elsewhere if you wish.

A good tip when working out this part of your budget is to divide the maximum you want to spend on providing refreshments by the number of guests that you have. This will then give you the amount that you can spend per head – it's a lot easier to work this way than to spend your time continually multiplying costs of starters or toast drinks. Now all you have to do is use the information that your venue has provided to construct a food and drink package that's both attractive and financially acceptable to you both.

Food Options

You really can cater on any budget at all and I have listed a quick overview of the main options that are open to you. Clearly, the number of guests that you hope to invite will have an impact, so do take this into consideration. It is generally expected that some form of food will be provided for those attending the wedding but you still have a great deal of flexibility in what you can serve so don't feel that there are guidelines that you must follow here. Also look at the structure of the day and your planned timings as discussed in Chapter 6. If the day is a long one with an early ceremony and a late party, you obviously can't let guests go hungry so you might want to compromise with an afternoon tea and a more substantial evening buffet or barbecue. Alternatively, a later ceremony with no additional evening guests might make a longer dinner more practical. So, here are your options.

A Fully Served Dinner

These can vary from a traditional two- or three-course meal to a gigantic feast depending on your budget. One thing you must consider is that you're trying to feed a large group of people with different tastes. You may wish to pick something adventurous but think carefully before choosing something that might not appeal to many guests – if no-one eats it, it's a waste of your money and your guests will spend the rest of the reception with rumbling stomachs! Often, it's more practical to pick a 'safe' meal which, whilst it might not be something you'd necessarily choose in a restaurant, will be a dish that your guests will eat. It's good always to provide a vegetarian option and you may have to liaise with your venue over choices for people with other dietary requirements.

Do ask your guests early on if they have any food allergies or intolerances to ensure that your venue can cater for their needs successfully. Another point is to consider when you're getting married – a bowl of wintery soup might not appeal in high summer, while a warming pud might be a good idea in winter. Some brides don't like the notion of soup as a starter in case of spillages on the dress but you could compromise here by having a 'light' colour soup such as parsnip so a little splash wouldn't be as noticeable as tomato! If you want a sit-down meal, you'll need to construct a seating plan so everyone

FOOD AND DRINK

knows where to go. This is essential to make sure that everyone receives the right meal. A sit-down meal also gives guests a good opportunity to relax for a few hours before the entertainments, which can be a very welcome relief in a long day, while one that is fully served feels quite decadent.

Price range – high

Sit-down and Buffet Mix

This is a good way to provide a wider choice of food as a main course but also retain the feeling of being pampered that goes with being waited on! Basically, guests are served their starter and can then help themselves from a buffet for their main course. They can then either be served desserts or provided with another buffet selection. You will probably still need a seating plan for this type of meal so people are in the right places for their starters.

Price range – medium to high

Buffet

Buffets can often be cheaper than sit-down meals but they're not just sandwiches and sausage rolls either. You can have a number of hot dishes – chicken, fish, other meats, salads, vegetables and vegetarian options. If you do want to try something adventurous, this is a good way to do it as most people will be able to find something they'll eat from such a large selection. If you are having a buffet, you can throw away the seating plan and just let people pick their own seats once they've chosen their food or still have a plan if you'd prefer. One thing to consider is the amount of time it can take everyone to serve themselves from a buffet (30 minutes plus for a medium-sized wedding) and this might not be ideal if you're pushed for time. If you have a large guest list, it is worth asking your venue if they can set up a number of buffet tables or 'stations' so that more people can be serving themselves at any one time.

Price range – low to medium

Canapés

If you don't want a large meal at this point (for example if you're planning a larger evening buffet or barbecue), canapés could provide the answer. Waiting staff mingle with the guests with trays of food for the guests to pick at. You need to choose non-crumbling, non-dripping foods that are easy to hold and come in bitesize portions. If you want hot canapés, try and serve them on little forks or with sticks. The 'average' guide is to provide 12–15 pieces per head and you should aim for 8–10 different choices. Again, you'll need some meat-free nibbles and make sure that staff can give guests more information about each canapé if asked. This is a great option if you want to eat and mingle or if you've got a relatively short day planned. Canapés are often served during the drinks reception, but if you're having a later ceremony, they can be circulated before the vows. This works really well because it ensures everyone arrives in plenty of time and can mean that you don't have to provide food again until the evening.

Price range – low

Alternative Feasts

If you want something a little different to the above, you could think about the following – afternoon teas (delicate sandwiches, pastries, cakes and scones), barbecue (lots of 'friendly' food and maybe even a few cooked-to-order specialities served with salads and breads) or even hog roasts (a real spectacle with guests being served succulent roast meat from a spit).

Price range – low to high, it's up to you!

As you can see, there are lots of ways that you can serve your food and, if you're a bit clever about your timings and plans, guests can feel suitably satisfied at any point and on any budget. It's not about throwing more than you can afford at the catering, it's about being logical about cost and thinking creatively about your plans. Sometimes, shaking things up a

FOOD AND DRINK

little can mean that instead of trying to force down a three-course meal at three in the afternoon in the summer heat, guests can take the edge off their hunger with some canapés and wait until later for an atmospheric and enjoyable hog roast. Don't feel that you have to conform to the wedding norm if you don't want to and don't be afraid to put your own stamp on the proceedings.

Cake

Wedding cakes are traditionally three-tier fruit cakes – the bottom two tiers are usually eaten on the day itself, or given to guests to take home or to those who could not attend, while the top layer is saved for the christening following the birth of the couple's first child. It makes a wonderful centrepiece and 'the cutting of the cake' is quite a highlight of the reception.

More and more couples are choosing to do things a little differently here too and there's now quite a variety of choices. While fruit cakes are traditional, many couples are deciding against them and having modern alternatives such as sponge, chocolate, carrot, banana or any combination of the above! If you want a good compromise to please both the traditionalists and the younger people, you can choose to have the bottom tier made of fruit and the other tiers made of any variety you choose. Fruit cake does have the benefit of being very rich so portions are quite small, but if you know it's unlikely to get eaten, does that matter? Some couples also have a 'cutting' or 'kitchen' cake so the display cake is made of one variety whilst there's another behind the scenes that can be served as well to provide a bit of choice.

When it comes to decorating your cake, these days there are no limits! You can have a classical white or ivory iced cake or you can go for a chocolate ganache covering (be sure to keep this somewhere cool as this can melt in warmer weather or even under lights!). You can have humorous marzipan or icing figures, crystal toppers or sugar flowers. The choice is yours.

If you want something more 'out of the ordinary' you'll probably need to find a wedding cake specialist who can create your design. If you prefer something plainer, supermarkets can supply the more traditional cakes (which keeps costs down) and others can sell you plainly iced cakes for you to decorate with flowers, ribbons or whatever takes your fancy. A cake bought from a supermarket can cost under £100 while for other creations the sky's the limit. However an average cost would be approximately £400. Remember that if you're stacking your cake, the bottom tier needs to be able to support the weight of those on top so piling fruit layers onto a sponge base might result in a collapsed cake.

TAMRYN'S TIP

Portion sizes do differ from fruit to sponge and you'll need approximately 2.25kg/5lb of fruit cake per 50 guests. A 2.25kg/5lb sponge cake would feed 25–30 guests.

If you want to keep your top tier after the wedding to celebrate the patter of tiny feet in the future, you really need a fruit cake. The icing must be removed and also the marzipan as the oils in this can go off if stored. If you're planning on using it within 18 months, wrap it in acid-free tissue paper and store it in a cardboard box rather than an airtight tin so it doesn't 'sweat' and put the box in a cool room, away from sunlight. Should you think that a longer storage period is required, wrap it in tin foil, then in two layers of freezer bags and pop it in the freezer and it will be fine for up to two years. Of course, if you don't want any cake afterwards, make sure that your venue knows to cut and serve everything during the evening and you can ask them to wrap leftovers in napkins for guests to take home.

The cutting of the cake usually takes place after dessert and before the speeches. This gives waiting staff time to take the cake away, cut it during the speeches and then serve it with coffee or during the evening. Of course, if you want to cut your cake later in the evening, that's absolutely fine too. In fact, using the cake cutting as the official start of your evening reception is brilliant because it brings additional guests into the celebrations straight away and means that your cake gets a little longer on display. It's also a nice idea to send cake to people who were unable to attend and you can buy cake boxes on the high street or order cake boxes with your names and the date printed on them for this purpose.

Alternatives to Cake

There are plenty of alternatives if you just don't want a cake or fancy something different as a centrepiece. For example, you could go for a croquembouche (a tower of choux buns encased in spun sugar), a mound of profiteroles covered in sauce or cream, a massive chocolate gateaux, fresh fruits artfully arranged or a huge Swiss roll with mouthwatering fillings. Individually stacked cup cakes are very fashionable as are portion-sized fruit or chocolate tarts.

TAMRYN'S TIP

Check who will provide your cake stand and cake knife. Some venues include this whilst others charge for it. You might even want to hire a suitable stand yourself from a cake maker or supplier.

These options could help keep costs down as they could be served to guests instead of dessert. If you're not a lover of cake, choosing something different means that you get what you like! Cheese cakes are also increasingly popular – wheels of cheese are stacked to form a 'cake' and are then used in lieu of dessert or as an evening buffet centrepiece along with fresh breads and crackers. There are some great cheese companies that can help you select the perfect varieties and costs are comparable with sweet cakes.

Drinks

You'll need to provide some form of drinks at your reception, even if it's just water and fruit juice otherwise you'll have lots of dehydrated guests! A little tipple will get everyone in the mood for a celebration and it is always nice to have a drink with food. You'll also need something for the toasts if you're planning on having them.

There are basically two options for drink provision – you can either let your venue or caterer provide it or you can purchase your own for the day. Should you wish to provide your own, you will probably be charged 'corkage' (a fee levied by the venue for opening and serving your own drinks which is usually around £5 per bottle) so make sure that any potential savings are still as attractive after adding in any corkage fees. If you let your venue provide the drinks, you can be safe in the knowledge they'll have adequate supplies, but if you want to supply your own (possibly courtesy of a trip to France) you'll probably have a wider choice.

Whoever provides your drinks, you are likely to need some or all of the following.

Arrival Drinks

These are most commonly served after the ceremony and before any food, during the photographs or on arrival at your reception venue. The traditional alcoholic choices include champagne, Bucks Fizz or sherry but if you want something slightly more unusual, kir royale, Pimms, gin and tonic or even mulled wine would be tasty alternatives. You should also provide something for the non-drinkers and children. A fruit punch or a sparkling fruit cordial would be good options here.

Drinks with the Meal

Some form of wine is usually served at this point, either red, white or both depending on your budget. Again, you'll need a non-alcoholic variety and maybe even mineral waters. If you don't want to pay for mineral waters, ask your venue to provide jugs of tap water which could be decorated with fruit, edible flowers or just served with lots of ice cubes.

Toasts

Although champagne is traditional here, it's not essential now that there are so many excellent sparkling wines. A sparkling cordial would make sure that the non-drinkers don't feel left out of the merriment. If you're planning to have the speeches before the meal, you'll need to make sure that the drinks are poured as guests are being seated so you can be ready to start promptly.

Amount of Drink

When you're working out your figures, you'll need to calculate how many bottles of wine you'll need and the general rule of thumb is that each guest will consume roughly half a bottle of wine with the meal and will need one glass for the toast. A bottle of champagne should give roughly six glasses or 12 if mixed to make Bucks Fizz. It's better to over-estimate than under- but check your venue's policy on refunds for bottles that aren't opened. If you pay for a set number of bottles and they're not all opened, ask for the remainder to be served to evening guests on their arrival or to be put behind the bar or on tables later. Of course, there's no rule saying that you have to provide that much wine for guests if you don't want to or if you don't have the funds. If you prefer, perhaps provide one glass and then make sure that the bar is open so that guests can purchase their own.

What you provide with regards to other drinks is entirely up to you. You may wish to provide an open bar where you'll pick up the tab at the end of the evening for all the drinks your guests have (you'll look wonderfully generous but this is open to abuse) or you can have a cash bar where guests pay for their own drinks (absolutely fine but give people notice so they bring enough money with them). An 'in-between' option is to provide each guest with a 'drinks voucher' that entitles them to spend a certain amount after which they have to pay themselves or to only provide a few options such as beer, soft drinks and a couple of spirits and orders outside of those must be paid for. Again, this is a question that only you can answer!

Some couples are against paying for unlimited drinks for all their guests whilst some feel that asking guests to pay for drinks is just not right. Whatever you decide, you need to ensure that your venue is fully aware of your plans and knows when to open the bar. Check whether your venue will allow guests to pay for drinks via credit or debit card and, if necessary, it might be prudent to warn people to make sure they bring adequate cash with them (particularly if there are no cash machines in the vicinity). There is always a great debate regarding the rights and wrongs of cash and pay bars at weddings but only you know your budget and your feelings, so as long as you are happy with your decision, that should be all that matters.

Caterers

As we saw in Chapter 5, there are a huge number of venues available and quite a few of those aren't hotels or other establishments with chefs and kitchens in house. Should your venue be one of these, you will need to bring in a caterer to provide, prepare and serve your food and drink.

As food at your wedding is important, regardless of your budget, take your time to find a fabulous caterer. Do lots of research and request information from those you feel are suitable. You should receive sample menus and quotations from at least three companies before you choose and possibly go for a tasting to sample the goods – I could write a menu that sounds mouthwatering but in reality you would be served with something completely different! Finding a caterer through personal recommendation is always good, but otherwise ask for references and follow them up to make sure the food is as good as the menu looks.

You should check the following with your caterers:

* Does the price include tables/chairs/table linen/ glasses/crockery/cutlery/serving staff/clearing up? If they do supply crockery etc., you might want to ask to see it before the day – if it's not to your taste or if it doesn't go with the 'look' of your day, you might like to consider hiring these items.
* How many staff will they bring with them?
* Does the price include bread and butter? Some companies will just supply this and then charge you for 'extras'.
* Is the cost given per person rather than per plate (otherwise you'll be charged if people want seconds)?
* Is VAT/service charge included in the quote? Are tips expected?
* Insurance – what do they have and are you expected to pay for any breakages or damages?
* Portion sizes, particularly for buffets, as the worst thing would be for food to run out before everyone has been served.
* Will you have to pay for food for their staff?
* Do they bring all their own equipment or will you need to hire any items for them such as fridges?

* Is there anything that they must have access to such as electricity or water? This is particularly important if you're planning a marquee wedding. Your marquee company should also be aware that you're bringing in caterers as it will help them to design adequate working space.

TAMRYN'S TIP

Confirm the points above and the cost both verbally and in writing before you book with your caterer. If there are any changes to your plans, let them know as soon as you can.

You will need to let your caterers know the following:

* The location of your reception and the date and time.
* Your budget per head and estimated guest numbers. You'll have to confirm numbers before the event and these numbers will determine your final costs. If guests don't manage to attend on the day, you'll still be charged for their meals.
* Special dietary requirements of any guests.
* Facilities that are available at your venue for them.
* Whether you would also like them to provide drinks and a bar facility.

Good caterers get booked up very early. If you're planning on using caterers, making these arrangements should be high on your priority list. There is more information on researching and choosing suppliers in Chapter 15.

Arrangements for Dinner _____

Aside from the food, there are plenty of other arrangements that need to be made for dinner and the construction of the seating plan is often right up there with the guest list for pre-wedding headaches! You want to make sure that your guests get on and enjoy talking to the people around them but you might not want to just 'clump' families together.

The main focus during the meal is the top table. Traditionally, this is a long table, facing the rest of the room where the bridal couple and immediate bridal party sits. From left to right (as you face the table) there should be the bridesmaid, father of the groom, mother of the bride, groom, bride, father of the bride, mother of the groom and best man. It's not usual for ushers or the partners of the bridesmaid and best man to also sit at the top table. However, 'rules' are made to be broken and you can adapt your top table to suit your family circumstances or do away with it all together as you could seat the members of the traditional top table all around your room as 'hosts' on each table. Likewise, if you don't want the feeling of everyone staring at you, opt for a round table rather than a long one but if you do that, make sure speakers move during the speeches so they can be seen and heard.

Guest Tables _____

Regarding the guest tables, tradition says that the closer family members should be seated on tables closest to the top table. If you don't want to do this, however, don't! Just spread everyone out so there's no obvious 'pecking order'. Another thing you could think about to avoid the inevitable 'I'm only on table number 6 while they're on table number 2' moan is to do away with numbers altogether and give your tables names instead (you can choose anything – famous couples, places you've been on holiday or are going on honeymoon, words for 'love' in various languages or words around your wedding theme if you have one). However, some couples are reverting to numbers because they feel that whatever they've called a table, it's still rather obvious as to whether or not it's close to the top table!

Think about the Mix

Etiquette says married couples shouldn't sit together at weddings but be spaced around the table. However, most people ignore this advice and keep couples together. With a little thought, it's not too tough to mix relatives, friends and colleagues if you seat complementing personalities together (and if they're part of a couple, they'll probably want the 'other half' to talk to)! Think carefully about where you place single people or guests who don't know any other guests – try to sit them near someone you know will make an effort to get them to join in the conversation. As tempting as it can be, don't finalise your seating plan too far in advance in case of any last-minute changes. If you've spent a long time arranging everything, it would be infuriating to have to re-work it. You will need to give a copy of the plan showing exactly who sits next to whom to your venue or whoever will be setting up your tables, to ensure that everything is as you've planned. If you've spent some time working things out, you want to be confident that this time won't be wasted.

Of course, you'll need to let guests know where they're sitting after all this hard work and your table plan should be displayed at the entrance to the reception room. It should be large enough so that people don't have to stand right in front of it to find their names. If you have a lot of guests, you might want to consider having two seating plans to avoid having a crowd around one chart or you might wish to opt for seating cards. These show the name of the guest and their table assignment, but as each card is individual, they can be picked up and taken away which avoids bottlenecks around the entrance to dinner. There is more about seating cards in Chapter 14.

CHAPTER CHECKLIST

The arrangements for everything concerning your food and drink should now be finalised – or at least you will know more about your options! If you take anything from this chapter, let it be the following:

❋ Don't feel that you have to provide limitless food and drink throughout the day.

❋ If you think carefully about the running order of your wedding, you can be more creative about what is served at which point.

❋ There's more to cake than simply fruit and make sure that you either store leftovers properly or that it's eaten or given away on the day.

❋ Remember to cater for people with special dietary requirements or those that don't drink in your plans.

❋ Working out how much you can spend per head early on will let you easily finalise a menu and drinks package to suit your budget.

❋ Spend some time devising your seating plan because it's great to see everyone laughing and chatting during refreshments, whatever you decide to provide.

Eight
The Wedding Party

The people that you choose to be a part of your wedding day can have a big impact on both your stress levels and the success of the day. It's all too easy to get carried away and ask everyone and anyone to be a bridesmaid or an usher but, as calculating as it sounds, you need to think carefully about who you want to ask. The roles of best man and chief bridesmaid are undeniably big jobs so you need people who will be able to take on the tasks and be as helpful as possible. A good chief bridesmaid or best man can make the lives of the bride and groom much easier in the run-up to the day and on the day itself. Someone who's not known for their reliability, punctuality or level-headedness might not be the best choice, however much you love them.

It's quite possible that you had an idea about the people you wanted to ask to join the wedding party even before you got engaged – perhaps you've been friends since school, they're related to either yourself or your partner or maybe you've been a part of their wedding previously. Before you pop the question, read through the job descriptions in this chapter and see if they're really cut out for the role.

Of course, the more people that are involved in the wedding party, the more the costs increase for outfits, flowers, buttonholes and even hair and make-up, so in each section there's a little list detailing the associated costs for each person. Some couples cover all of those costs themselves and some pay for part, but whichever route you choose it is up to you and your budget. However, it's best to clarify these points very early on because for some people, the expense might be a problem. Even if cost isn't an issue, it's always a good idea to let those involved know where they stand sooner rather than later to avoid problems at a later date.

Asking the Question

Once you have decided who you would like to be a part of the wedding party, you get the wonderful job of actually asking them. It can be nice to make an effort with this to make people feel special from the outset. Of course, the more enthusiastic you can get them about the day, the more help they are likely to give you. Some people send a card, some send chocolate or flowers with a suitable note and some just like to ask face to face over a drink or a meal.

A couple of my favourite ideas that we have used for clients are personalised jigsaws, diaries or calendars. The jigsaws can easily be ordered from photo processors and can be images of you and the person that you wish to ask, or anything that you think is suitable, with the words 'will you be my bridesmaid?' or similar printed on top. When the jigsaw is put together, the question is asked! The diary idea is even simpler – get a blank diary for the year in question and just write on the day you have fixed for your wedding 'Be Bridesmaid' and place the ribbon marker in that page. We have also sent out boxes full of cut-out letters that when arranged spell the question, so the only limit is your imagination. None of these ideas are incredibly expensive but they are all very effective which is far more important than the cost.

Here is a run-down of the wedding party's roles, both before, during and after the wedding day.

Best Man

The choice of the best man is really down to the groom. As it's a job that involves lots of work and responsibility, it's not a decision to be made lightly. As with the bride's chief bridesmaid or maid of honour, the best man's job is to take some pressure off the groom so the ideal candidate needs to be organised, dependable and confident. If you're going to have speeches, the best man's is quite a focal point and having someone who's not nervous about this aspect of the day can be very beneficial. Punctuality is another major factor as it's really the best man who is responsible for the groom on the morning of the wedding. The best man does have quite a lot of tasks to perform on the day, even after the ceremony, so he'll need to be aware of these in advance. If you have not got a wedding day co-ordinator, much of the onus for timekeeping and supplier liaison falls to the best man which means he will need to be very au fait with your plans.

Once you have picked 'The Very Best Man' for the job, give him this list to make him realise the extent of his task!

Before the Wedding

* Helps the groom to choose any ushers or other 'groomsmen'.
* Arranges the hire or purchase of the men's outfits.
* Attends any pre-wedding meetings at the venue or with other suppliers.
* Confirms all arrangements for the day by liaising with the bride and groom and their families as necessary.
* Arranges the stag party. He should make sure it's something that the groom is happy to do and also ensure that the groom returns home unscathed after the event!
* Attends the ceremony rehearsal, if applicable.

On the Day

* Makes sure the luggage needed for the honeymoon is at the venue or in a safe place.
* Checks and distributes the buttonholes.
* Organises the ushers and makes sure they have the orders of ceremony, confetti or anything else that is to be handed to the guests.
* Double-checks that any parking arrangements or other plans made for guests are in order.
* Makes any payments that are necessary on the day on behalf of the groom – i.e., registrar's fees, final payments to DJs or bands.
* Helps the groom to get ready and gets him to the ceremony on time.
* Looks after the rings before the ceremony and hands them over at the correct point.
* Walks out after the ceremony with the maid of honour or chief bridesmaid.
* Helps the photographers to gather guests for the photographs.
* Ensures that all guests can get to the reception (if at another venue) before he leaves himself.
* Makes sure that any items needing to be transported between venues are moved at the right moment.
* Generally looks after guests and mingles with them before the dinner.
* Tries to ensure that things happen on time and schedules don't overrun.
* Deals with any wedding presents brought to the venue and makes sure that they are in a safe place.
* Announces the entrance of the bride and groom into dinner and the cutting of the cake.
* Introduces the speeches and makes one himself.
* If the bride and groom are leaving the reception, the best man should take charge of the groom's clothes, make sure the groom has all the correct travel

documents, organise the guests to say goodbye to the couple and even decorate the going-away car.

After the Event

* Returns any hired clothes to the shop.
* Makes sure any gifts are safe for the bride and groom's return.
* Helps with any follow-up duties as requested.

Costs for the Best Man

* Suit hire costs are usually less than £100. If you add in the hire of shoes and other items, it can be more but a lot of suppliers offer discounts if all members of the party book together.
* A buttonhole for the best man will cost around £5, depending on the flowers used and the size. One option is to scrap buttonholes altogether and go for coloured pocket squares instead – these can often be hired with the suits and won't wilt or get crushed during the day.
* Lots of couples buy the best man some kind of gift to thank him for his assistance and involvement and these can be anything from a small token to a larger item, depending on available funds.

Chief Bridesmaid or Matron/Maid of Honour

This role usually goes to the bride's closest female friend or maybe even a relation. The duties here are not unlike those of the best man and also involve quite a reasonable amount of work. The best quality a chief bridesmaid or matron/maid of honour can have is patience – she'll probably need to listen to the bride ranting and raving over her wedding plans/family/husband-to-be on more than one occasion and there will be plenty of dress-hunting expeditions too. As emotions on the morning of the wedding are often running a little high, having someone by your side who is a calming influence is important. You can never be sure what will crop up in the run-up to the day so having a chief bridesmaid or matron/maid of honour that you feel you can totally rely on is very reassuring.

Before the Wedding
* Goes dress-hunting with the bride for all of the female outfits.
* Organises the hen party and takes care of the bride during it!
* Attends dress fittings for herself and the bride.
* Tries to undertake any little jobs that will make the bride's life a little easier. These could be anything from addressing invitation envelopes to wrapping favours or gifts.
* Goes to any rehearsals that have been organised.

On the Day
* Checks that all the females' bouquets are ready.
* Helps the bride to get ready and also assists any other bridesmaids or flower girls.
* Makes sure that everyone leaves for the ceremony on time. If going by car, the chief bridesmaid or matron/maid of honour will usually travel with the mother of the bride and any other attendants but obviously that is dependant on circumstances.
* Double-checks that the bride is looking radiant before she makes her way up the aisle.
* Either walks in before or after the bride depending on what she decides to do.
* Holds the bride's bouquet during the ceremony and assists her to lift her veil if appropriate.
* Keeps an eye on any other attendants during the ceremony.
* Walks out with the best man.

* Helps to greet guests and make them feel welcome.
* Deals with presents or cards along with the best man.
* Ensures that the bride has make-up to reapply for the photographs if necessary.
* If the bride and groom are leaving the reception she may also help the bride to change and takes care of her dress while she's away.

After the Event
* Be available to 'ooh' and 'aah' over the wedding photos and not be jealous of the bride's honeymoon tan!
* Undertakes any jobs as requested (e.g., returning hired items to suppliers).

Costs for the Chief Bridesmaid or Matron/Maid of Honour
* The dress is certainly the largest cost and finding a dress for less than £150 is tricky. Of course, some dresses are much more expensive depending on the designer.
* Accessories such as shoes, jewellery and a tiara or other headdress can easily add another £100, if not more.
* A bridesmaid's bouquet will usually start at around £40–50 but can be more depending on the flowers and size chosen.
* The traditional gift given to the chief bridesmaid or matron/maid of honour is their jewellery for the day but some couples also give another gift during the speeches.

Ushers

The general role of the ushers is to help guests as they enter and leave the ceremony. Their role doesn't generally extend into the reception, so it's perfectly fine to have younger ushers although you may like to have one older one to keep an eye on them all! Having said that, if you have ushers that can help round up guests required for photos and help people into dinner at the appropriate time, the day will run much more smoothly. Ushers also need to be reliable but perhaps not to the same extent as the best man. Choosing ushers that know quite a few of the guests can make seating at the ceremony easier, but generally just choosing ushers who are happy to get involved is the best idea.

Before the Wedding
  * Go for clothes fittings if required.
  * Get details of any guests who need special attention at the ceremony and also find out if there is any reserved seating for VIPs.
  * Ask the bride and groom to provide them with large umbrellas on the day to make sure no-one gets rained on should the weather not be perfect.
  * Attend the rehearsal if required.

On the Day
  * Arrive at the ceremony venue early to help with any last-minute arrangements.
  * Go through the timings and plan for the ceremony with the best man.
  * Assist guests with parking if required.
  * Greet guests as they enter the ceremony room and hand them an order of ceremony or whatever else is being provided.
  * Escort the bride's and groom's parents to their seats.
  * Ensure that any seating plans for close family are followed.
  * Place an order of ceremony on seats for the bridesmaids, bride and groom.
  * Traditionally, the ushers would seat the bride's family on the left and the groom's on the right but they should use their judgement to make sure one side doesn't look cramped and the other empty.

* Make sure that any guests giving readings have copies of the reading concerned and are seated so that they can get out of their row easily.
* Try to seat families with younger children near the exits or at ends of rows.
* Assist the best man after the ceremony in marshalling guests for photos.
* In the event of rain, help to shelter the bride and groom, other attendants and immediate family.

After the Event
* Return any hired clothing as soon as possible.

Costs of Ushers
* Suit hire costs are usually less than £100. If you add in the hire of shoes and other items, it can be more but a lot of suppliers offer discounts if all members of the party book together.
* A buttonhole for each usher will cost around £5, depending on the flowers used and the size. As with the best man, pocket squares could be used instead of floral buttonholes.
* Lots of couples buy the ushers a gift and these are usually smaller than the gift given to the best man.

Bridesmaids, Flower Girls and Page Boys

An older bridesmaid would maybe take a more active role in the day or even share some of the chief bridesmaid or matron/maid of honour's tasks. However, younger bridesmaids, page boys and flowers girls generally don't have any designated tasks other than to be in the right place at the right time (which can still be a nightmare!). If you're only having younger attendants, it might be wise to enlist one or two people to keep them under control!

Before the Wedding

* Discuss outfits with the bride and go for fittings as required.
* Find out from the bride exactly what's required on the day.

On the Day

* Arrive dressed at the venue in plenty of time, and get any last-minute instructions from the chief bridesmaid or matron/maid of honour.
* Walk up the aisle behind the chief bridesmaid or matron/maid of honour.
* Stand or sit during the ceremony as arranged.
* Walk out after the chief bridesmaid or matron/maid of honour and best man.
* A page boy or flower girl may be designated the 'ringbearer' and will be called forward to give the rings to the celebrant at the right moment.
* A flower girl may be required to walk ahead of the bride and groom to throw flower petals onto the floor before them.
* Be available for photographs.

After the Event

* Give back any hired clothing as soon as possible.

Costs of the Bridesmaids

* As with the chief bridesmaid or matron/maid of honour, dresses can be a large cost and finding a dress for less than £150 will be difficult. Dresses for younger bridesmaids can be bought for a more reasonable cost on the high street.
* Accessories such as shoes, jewellery and a tiara or other headdress can easily add another £100, if not more. However, accessories for children do cost less.

* A bridesmaid's bouquet will usually start at around £40–50 but can be more depending on the flowers and size chosen. Smaller bridesmaids are often given much smaller bouquets to carry or even baskets filled with flowers.
* Bridesmaids are often given jewellery before the ceremony as a gift from the bride but some receive other gifts so it's up to you!

Parents of the Bride and Groom

It is really the bride's parents that have the more important role on the day as traditionally they are the 'hosts' of the event and the bride's father will often escort his daughter up the aisle as well as making a speech. The groom's parents have much less involvement as they are technically guests at the wedding but if you would like them to play more of a part in the day, go ahead and involve them.

Before the Wedding

* Assist with the planning as requested by the bride and groom and possibly have some input into the guest list and other arrangements.

On the Day

* The bride's father can accompany his daughter up the aisle. He should walk on her right-hand-side and 'hand' his daughter to the groom before stepping back and taking his seat.
* The bride's father and the groom's mother followed by the bride's mother and the groom's father should walk down the aisle together following the ceremony.
* Both sets of parents can take part in a receiving line.
* The bride's parents should welcome guests to the reception.

THE WEDDING PARTY

After the Day

❋ The bride's parents may send out cake to people who couldn't attend while the bride and groom are on honeymoon.

Costs of the Parents

❋ The father of the bride and even the father of the groom are often dressed in the same suits as the groom, best man and ushers so hire costs apply here too.

❋ Buttonholes are frequently provided for the fathers and more elaborate corsages are often ordered for the mothers. Corsages are more expensive than standard buttonholes because of the size involved.

TAMRYN'S TIP

When ordering corsages from your florist, ask that they are made with magnetic attachments rather than pins which sometimes can't hold the weight of the corsage and often begins to rip finer fabrics on women's outfits.

Witnesses and Readers

These are important people and although they're not really classed as part of the wedding party, choosing your witnesses and readers is another great job. It gives you an opportunity to include other friends or family members who haven't been given one of the roles mentioned previously or you could ask your best man or bridesmaid to also be a witness. Witnesses sign the marriage entry in the legal register and you'll need two (although some officiants will let you have up to four but do confirm this). Legally, your witnesses have to both see and hear you take your vows so they will need to be seated close to the front, possibly on the end of an aisle to make it easy for them to come forward when it's time for them to sign the register with you both. There's no legal age requirement for witnesses although they do have to be old enough to understand the solemnity of the vows you are making so most tend to be over 16.

Readings are a brilliant way to personalise your ceremony (as discussed in Chapter 4) and your readers will have to be comfortable about performing this task. Standing up and reading in front of a large crowd of people isn't everyone's idea of fun so if someone you ask really doesn't feel up to it, don't be upset. Perhaps they could take on another job for you – see some ideas below.

Costs of Witnesses and Readers

* There's no need to worry about costs for outfits but some couples do provide buttonholes for these guests. However, that's not essential by any stretch of the imagination.

* It's becoming more popular to buy a gift for witnesses and readers but it's not expected. Most would be happy to be bought a drink later in the evening or maybe ask your photographer to take a photo of them 'in action' so that you can order a copy at a later date to send with a thank-you letter.

Other VIPs and Alternatives

Of course there are plenty of other important people than those listed above, particularly grandparents, other close relations or friends. Although there's no specific job for these people, lots of couples still like to find ways to include them in the day as suggested by the following.

Master of Ceremonies

Having a friend or family member introduce you both into dinner and announce the speeches can be a great idea. Obviously, this person needs to be pretty confident and loud enough to speak to a large group of people. You might like to provide them with a buttonhole, corsage or gift but it's not strictly necessary.

Additional Reading

This is a particularly cunning way to get around the rules surrounding readings with a religious element if you're having a civil ceremony. Someone could give another reading before dinner or at an appropriate moment at the reception, which won't be covered by the restrictions imposed on the ceremony.

Talented Guests

Some guests might have a talent that could bring something to your day. Asking someone who's great with flowers to make you a very personal bouquet, for example, would be brilliant. Just make sure that they are comfortable with the responsibility before you get too carried away!

Ultimately, you know your friends and family best, so don't be shy about bringing them into the celebrations. As long as everyone is clear as to what is expected, there shouldn't be any problems.

Alternative Wedding Parties

Of course, you don't have to follow the 'traditional' wedding party pattern if it doesn't suit you. Popular twists on the norm are a 'best woman' instead of a best man, if the groom has a close female friend, or a 'bride's man' in lieu of a chief bridesmaid or matron/ maid of honour. Some people might raise an eyebrow at this but it's imperative that you surround yourself with the people that you want on the big day, not those who fit stereotypes. Actually, these twists can work really well – the best man's speech with a feminine touch can miss out the risqué jokes that offend all too easily and the bride's man seems to stop any over-the-top bridal moments! Likewise, there's no rule saying that a bride can only be given away by her father and some choose to be accompanied by both parents. Ushers don't have to be male and you don't need to ask every child in the family to be a flower girl. Consider carefully the people that are most important to you, not lists saying what is 'expected'.

Speeches

Speeches are an integral part of the reception and traditionally run in the following order – father of the bride, groom and the best man. However, more and more brides are choosing to say a few words too and their speech can be slotted in either before or after the groom's. Some brides of course like to get 'the last word' and speak after the best man! This is particularly effective if the groom isn't expecting his new wife to stand up. It's not unknown for a relative of the groom to make a speech as well, but do be careful that things don't run on too long with numerous speakers. Even the most attentive guests can't help but allow their attention to wander after half an hour!

By making a speech, people who have helped make the day a success can be thanked in public and it's an opportunity to amuse and entertain the guests with 'witty' comments about the bride and groom. Speeches are also a 'lead in' to the toasts where everyone present can wish you both well. In this section we'll give some hints for each speaker and also give you tips on making a fabulous speech.

The Bride's Father
The purpose of this speech is to greet the guests, congratulate the happy couple and welcome the groom into the family. If

the bride's father isn't present, the person who gave her away or a close friend or relative could make this speech instead. The speaker may like to include some funny stories about the bride when she was younger, comment on how fantastic she looks today and even offer a few words of wisdom to the newlyweds. The speech should end with a toast to 'the bride and groom', 'the happy couple' or even 'Mr and Mrs ...'

The Groom

He should start by thanking the bride's father for making him feel part of the family and for their help in organising the wedding. He should also thank the guests for coming and for their generous gifts. A mention should also be made here of his parents and anyone else who has contributed to the wedding. The main focal point of the groom's speech, however, is his words about his new wife whether they're funny, affectionate or highly emotional – this is the point to show everyone how much he adores her! The groom's speech should end with a toast to the bridesmaids.

The Bride

As this is a little new, you basically have the freedom to say whatever you wish. You may like to make special mention of friends or family members who have been a particular help, you can give out gifts to wedding party members or just say a few words about your new husband. There is no 'set' toast for the bride to make but if you'd like to give a toast, you could toast to friends and family, to health and happiness, or anything that means something to you.

The Best Man

This is the speech with the most pressure! It's supposed to be funny, entertaining and slightly risqué! However, best men should think about the audience – Great Aunt Phyllis doesn't really need to hear about the stag night antics! His speech should also compliment the bridesmaids and thank the groom for his toast. He can also thank people who have helped out and he might like to say a few words about his relationship with the groom. It's appropriate for him to end his speech with a toast to the newlyweds.

One question that often arises with regards to the speeches is how to remember relatives who are no longer with you. The best advice is to keep it brief – a few gentle words mentioning how much they would have enjoyed the day or how happy they would have been to see everyone enjoying themselves is more than enough. A lighter section afterwards will shift the atmosphere again.

TAMRYN'S TIP

If you want to remember relatives but don't want to do it in a speech, you could write a few words about them on the menus or order of ceremony, place a photograph of them on the cake table or pick one of their favourite songs to be played during the ceremony or during the evening reception.

Making Good Speeches

Another frequently asked question is 'How do I make a good speech?' There are some tips in this section but the biggest thing to remember is that every single person in the room is on your side, they want you to do well and they're not going to criticise you if you make a little mistake.

✳ Do think about your speech beforehand – even just making notes on the areas you would like to cover is worthwhile.

* Don't fill your speech with nonsense just to make it longer – a fantastic minute-long speech is better than five minutes of 'average'.
* Don't drink much before your speech on the day – it won't make your speech sound any better to the audience!
* Use your normal voice – don't put on any airs and graces. Just relax, take a few deep breaths and speak as you would to friends.
* Don't race through your speech – make a mark on your notes to remind you to take a breather.
* If you mention anyone specifically, look at them, but don't stare at them for longer than necessary.
* Double-check any jokes with someone else – you might find them absolutely hilarious but others might not.
* Stand with your feet slightly apart to steady you and have your hands by your sides or holding your notes. Leaning on the table, putting your hands in your pockets or clenching your arms behind your back isn't good!

There are, of course, whole books dedicated to the subject of speeches (see Further Information at the back of this book), but as long as you speak from the heart, your speech will be a hit.

You're Not Alone

Sometimes, family circumstances such as divorced parents or a best man who likes a drink or eight can seem to be a huge problem when you are planning your wedding. One thing to bear in mind is that you are not alone. Plenty of other couples have had to deal with these worries and there are lots of ways that you can deal with any potential problems in advance. The modern flexibility surrounding weddings is very helpful as it's possible to omit or alter areas that might cause an unpleasant atmosphere. Some common dilemmas surrounding the bridal party and workable solutions are as follows:

Divorced Parents

Understandably, wondering how divorced parents will cope with the day can be a major concern, especially if new partners are involved too. It's very rare for people not to be able to swallow their feelings for one day, particularly when it should be such a happy occasion. If you have got parental problems, do let suppliers know so no-one tries to force ex-partners together for the sake of a photograph. Seating arrangements are another hot topic so we suggest that if parents are still on speaking terms or are prepared to put their own issues aside for the day, then the 'traditional' top table is still possible as they won't be sitting next to each other anyway! If you are incorporating new partners, they could be seated towards the ends of the top table or on guest tables. You could perhaps ditch the standard table arrangement and let parents play host at the other tables. This makes everyone feel special and it's good for guests as they get someone from the main wedding party sitting with them. Alternatively, have a 'bride and groom' table on your own or seat your bridesmaids, best man and ushers (along with partners if you like) with you both.

Not the Best Man

Lots of brides have concerns about the 'not so' best man! He might be a lovely chap and your partner's oldest friend but you also know that he likes a drink and has the tendency to get rather 'vocal' at times. Again, speaking to someone in the wedding group about your concerns can be a great help – fathers of the bride can be very effective here to keep someone in check, at least until the end of the formalities. Or, speak to someone at the venue, particularly whomever is announcing speeches so that they can step in at the right (but wrong!) moment if required. If people know how you want situations to be handled, they can deal with things on your behalf without making a fuss or bringing anyone else into the fray.

Suited and Booted?

With the shift to more informal celebrations, it can be really hard for the men in the wedding party to know what to wear. In fact, who in the wedding party should wear outfits similar to the groom? I would suggest that fathers, best men and ushers should stand out from the crowd a little – it makes it easier for guests to know who's in the wedding party – but you could easily differentiate between them by using different buttonholes, waistcoats, ties or cravats. They don't all have to look identical and sometimes giving men a little freedom is a good idea! Of course, you don't have to specify what socks they should wear, but if you can make sure they clean their shoes as photos of suited chaps walking together are really popular and scruffy shoes are noticeable.

Attention-free Attendants

This is a common complaint – you've chosen your bridesmaids and then they don't seem that bothered. You know there are dresses to be ordered and accessories to choose but they can never find the time for you. A lot of this can often be put down to the hectic pace at which we all live our lives these days and, as much as you would like it to be, your wedding doesn't always come top of everyone else's priority lists. So, when the excitement of the role is still new to your attendants, book in early for dress-shopping expeditions and hen nights. Planning in advance here can help to get things done and stop you feeling like people don't care. Make wedding tasks fun things that you can all look forward to for a while, not something you try to cram into packed diaries at the last moment.

CHAPTER CHECKLIST

The wedding party is an understandably large part of the day hence this rather sizeable chapter! The most important things to remember are:

✳ Take your time when choosing the wedding party. You need to be sure that the people involved are going to do a good job for you.

✳ Don't be afraid to do things differently from the 'standard' wedding party arrangements if that suits you, your family and friends best.

✳ Speeches are not as scary as you think they might be. Everyone is supporting the speakers, not judging them.

✳ There are plenty of ways to involve more people in the day. Just think creatively and get everyone in on the action.

✳ If you've got family 'issues', you are not the first and you won't be the last. Deal with things early on and delegate someone to keep an eye on potential flashpoints during the day itself for you so that you can relax.

Nine
The Guests

It has often been said that organising a wedding would be simple if it weren't for the guests and in some respects that's true! There wouldn't be any table-plan headaches, people failing to reply to your invitation, unexpected dietary requirements and, of course, it would be much less expensive! However, surely one of the main purposes of the day is to declare your love in front of your friends and family so the 'guest-free wedding' never actually materialises (even if you do wish for it on some of those sleepless nights!).

Looking back now at your notes from those early brainstorming sessions can be incredibly helpful at this point. You should have noted your preference for an intimate or large-scale event so keep this in mind when you begin work on your guest list. Keep referring back to those notes because this will help to ensure that your wedding is the day that you both wanted, not one that has evolved of its own accord without your agreement.

The Guest List

Deciding who will be there on your big day can be a big headache as everyone has their own views and restrictions from the venue to the bank manager which can often mean that someone is going to be upset at the outcome. Plus, when you add in possible parental pressure, it's easy to see why confirming the guest list can be one of the trickiest tasks that you'll be faced with whilst planning.

The first thing to do is to work out how many people you can invite to the whole day, including the ceremony and any post-ceremony celebrations such as drinks, canapés or dinner. You may need to think about how many invitations will be sent to 'evening reception only' guests. This is important if you are having a civil ceremony as there will be a limit on the amount of people who can be present. This is absolutely fixed as the venue's wedding licence will state the maximum number that can be in each approved room. Don't feel constrained by this figure, however, as it has the benefit of giving you a definitive number to work with. Without a number such as this, it's very easy to keep inviting 'just one more', which is how numbers (and of course costs) begin to spiral. If you have a little more flexibility (for example, with a church wedding), you will still need to come to a compromise between who you want to be there and who you can afford to have there.

Whatever budget you are working to and whatever style of day you're working to, there's no getting away from the fact that each additional name on your guest list will increase the cost of the day. If that's not a problem, that's great, but if it is, you need to think carefully about your list or reorganise your budget or plans. You might need to cut down, for example, on the amount of wine served during your meal to be able to accommodate some friends from school. Yet again, I'm going to have to tell you that there's no right way to do things in a situation like this – the only thing you should try to stick to is what's important to you. Again, check back on your brainstorming notes and remind yourself of what your priorities are if it's all becoming a bit confused.

Be a Little Ruthless

Once you've decided on, or found out how many places you have available, start by writing a list of 'the definite guests' – people you are totally sure you want to be with on the day such as close family and friends. Then, make a list of 'the optional guests' which can include people from work, family friends, distant relations and general acquaintances. You can also make a list of 'promotion prospects' – people who are only going to be invited to the reception but those you would also like to be at the ceremony if some of your 'definite guests' decline. It's a horribly calculating way to decide on who comes but it's impossible to invite everyone to everything and you have to reach some kind of compromise. Being a bit ruthless now can save you headaches later on, so it's worth it, however mercenary you might feel!

TAMRYN'S TIP

When you're working on the guest list, don't forget to include yourselves and the rest of the wedding party in your figures! It's easy to miss people out, which can make life very difficult, particularly when you're working to an absolute maximum limit for guest numbers.

In theory, the bride and groom should each have equal numbers of guests but this isn't always possible if one family is much larger than another. In this case, you need to reach an amicable compromise between you. Some couples half the total number of invitations between them and write their own lists for their family and friends, others start by listing those they jointly want to invite and dividing the remaining spaces between them whilst some work together on the entire list. Use whichever system you feel most comfortable with and try to enjoy the process because, however hard it may be, it's taking you a step closer to achieving the wedding that you discussed in those first planning conversations.

Sometimes, deciding who comes is not easy – you may be worried that you will offend people who aren't invited or you may get upset that you can't ask everyone you'd like. However, most people will realise that you're in a tricky situation with regards to numbers and are usually more understanding than you might imagine.

Children

The one guest list query that seems to create more problems than all the others combined is the issue of children – do you invite them or not? The answer to this question often lies in the kind of wedding that you're planning and your family situation. A small, sophisticated dinner or a very late party might not be suitable for children whereas a large family event would be. If you have a tight restriction on numbers on your guest list, inviting children will take up places and it can be hard keeping children amused (and therefore quiet) during the ceremony and a long dinner. But if you want children there, with a little planning, they can easily be entertained.

There are several 'solutions' to the issue of children – you can be strict and not invite any at all (which may offend some people), you can invite only children of close relatives (which may offend some friends) or you can invite them just to the reception. Whatever you decide, you need to make it clear on your invitation exactly who is invited in case some people assume that it's okay to bring their children. If you take a 'no children' approach, you may need to prepare yourself for some backlash and possible declines to your invitation because of it. However, some parents might be grateful for a day without their children where they can enjoy themselves without being on duty. Ultimately, you need to be consistent because if you have told parents 'no children' and yet they arrive on the day to see a few there, they may start to feel that their children were singled out and it will be seen more as a personal affront than a blanket decision.

Unfortunately, there is no right or wrong with regards to inviting children to a wedding (I wish there was!) and it's simply down to personal choice and your ability to see through your decision despite any problems that may occur because of it. Whatever you decide, you won't be alone because of all the questions that I get from clients, this is one of the most popular (or unpopular as the case may be.)! Again, keep reminding yourself that this is your day and as long as you're not being deliberately rude or hurtful, you should be entitled to celebrate your marriage in the way that you wish.

Invitations and Information

Your invitations are the first thing your guests see about your wedding so it's important to make a good impression. Here are some helpful hints for invitations with impact. If you can get your guests excited and interested in your wedding day from the word go, it's a great feeling (and can also help with getting those RSVPs back!)

Choosing Your Invitations

There are so many different types of invitations from formal to informal, handmade to personally printed, that it's tough to pick. My advice is to choose something that's 'you' – there's no point in having formal, engraved invitations if your wedding is going to be informal and modern. Also, think of your budget. If you'd rather spend the cash on other things, go for pre-printed invitations where you can just fill in your details or print some yourself from a PC. If you've got room in the budget, personally designed or hand-calligraphed invitations make a great statement. There are all sorts of ideas and suppliers covered in various websites and magazines, so do some research.

When to Order

Once you know your venue, dates and times you can order your stationery. If you're on a short timescale, you can buy 'fill in the blank' invitations from stationers. Remember that quite a lot of stationery businesses are small and can only deal with a certain number of orders so be sure to check their estimated delivery times before you order.

How Many to Order

You need one invitation for each person, couple or family. It's best to order a few spares too in case you make a mistake writing them. Even though all of your close family and wedding party will be well aware of the details of the day by this point, it's still nice to send invitations to the parents, bridesmaids, ushers and best man.

When to Send Them

Most guides say six weeks before is about right but if you're getting married in high summer, have people travelling from overseas or need to get final numbers to your venue or caterer by a certain point, you can send them well before this to make your life (and the lives of your guests) easier. More and more couples are sending out their invitations up to six months in advance and there's nothing wrong with this, especially if you want to give yourself time to invite other guests if you receive any declines from the first mailing. Decide what sending date is best for you and work to your own timescales.

RSVP Dates

The RSVP date that you set should be guided by the requirements of your venue or caterers because you'll need final numbers for them. Most venues need to know exact numbers attending two to four weeks before the day so add another couple of weeks onto that to allow you time to chase any late responses and make that your RSVP date. Make sure you confirm this cut-off date with your venue and caterers.

RSVP Cards

You can include pre-printed RSVP cards in your invitations so that guests can simply complete them and send them back but this obviously increases the cost of the invitations. Don't feel that you have to include an RSVP card and indeed lots of guests like to choose their own. It is still 'the done thing' to send a written RSVP in return to an invitation, but if you know that you're more likely to get speedy responses if you include an e-mail address, then go ahead. Getting all of your guests to respond to your invitation is always tricky and most couples have some outstanding replies at their RSVP date. Don't feel bad if you need to chase people to find out whether they're coming and don't make any assumptions!

Dressing Up

If you want your wedding guests to wear a certain something on your day, it's best to make this request on your invitation. An evening wedding, for example, could be a strictly black tie event or a themed wedding could include an element of fancy dress. It's up to you and whatever you request should be put in writing to avoid confusion rather than relying on word of mouth.

TAMRYN'S TIP

A good way to signal a dress code to your guests without dictating too much to them is to put something similar to 'Ladies – hats are more than welcome' on the invitation so everyone knows they've got the opportunity to dress up.

Do try, however, to avoid putting people under pressure with your dress code – for some, a black tie event is no problem but for others it's more stressful, so try not to opt for something that will make your guests uncomfortable or mean that they have to spend a lot of money on clothes for the day. Most people like to buy a new item or outfit for a wedding but that's their choice; it's another matter when they've been forced into it so be kind!

Writing and Wording Your Invitations

Invitations should be addressed formally e.g., Mr and Mrs D Smith rather than Uncle Dave and Auntie Sarah. Also, if you're following traditional etiquette, you should write an invitation for the groom's parents and the rest of the bridal party (but not the bride's parents if they're the hosts). You should also handwrite your envelopes rather than use printed labels. If this concerns you bear in mind that with computerised sorting systems, handwritten envelopes (complete with postcodes) often pass through the mail rooms speedily and safely.

As the invitations are usually sent by the 'hosts' of the wedding, their names appear at the top. The hosts are usually the bride's parents, irrespective of whether they're paying for everything, but you can have the hosts as anyone you like. Many couples now include their own names and those of both sets of parents. Every option shown below is much more acceptable now than it ever has been, so word your invitations to fit your wedding, as there's no need to stick to the accepted norm if you don't want to.

Religious Wedding

For a ceremony followed by a reception at another venue, you should give the locations and times for both e.g., 'Mr and Mrs P Sandy request the pleasure of the company of (space to enter guest's names) on the occasion of the marriage of their daughter Tamryn Sarah to Mr James T Kirby at St John the Evangelist, Woodley, on Saturday 1st March 2003 at 3pm and afterwards at Cliveden House, Maidenhead, for dinner and an evening reception at 5pm.'

Civil Wedding

For a civil wedding in an approved venue, you need only give the time of the ceremony and a few details of what will be happening afterwards e.g., 'Mr and Mrs P Sandy request the pleasure of the company of (space to enter guest's names) on the occasion of the marriage of their daughter Tamryn Sarah to Mr James T Kirby at Cliveden House, Maidenhead at 3pm. The ceremony will be followed by dinner and an evening reception.'

Bride's Parents as Hosts

Mr and Mrs P Sandy request the pleasure of the company of (space to enter guest's names) on the occasion of the marriage of Tamryn Sandy to Mr James T Kirby ...

Bride and Groom as Hosts

Tamryn Sandy and James Kirby request the pleasure of the company of (space to enter guest's name) on the occasion of their marriage ...

Divorced Parents

Mr Peter Sandy and Mrs Daphne Sandy request the company of (space to enter guest's names) on the occasion of the marriage of their daughter ...

Bride's Mother (Divorced)

Mrs Daphne Sandy requests the pleasure of the company of (space to enter guest's names) on the occasion of the marriage of her daughter ...

Divorced Parents (Bride's Mother Remarried)

Mr Peter Sandy and Mrs Daphne Eastment request the pleasure of the company of (space to enter guest's names) on the occasion of the marriage of their daughter ...

Bride's Mother Remarried

Mr and Mrs C Smythe request the pleasure of the company of (space to enter guest's names) on the occasion of the marriage of her daughter ...

Bride's Father Remarried

Mr and Mrs P Sandy request the pleasure of the company of (space to enter guest's name) on the occasion of the marriage of his daughter ...

Bride's Father as Host

Mr Peter Sandy requests the pleasure of the company of (space to enter guest's names) on the occasion of the marriage of his daughter ...

Bride's Mother as Host (or if Widowed)

Mrs P Sandy requests the pleasure of the company of (space to enter guest's name) on the occasion of the marriage of her daughter ...

Other Hosts

Mr and Mrs F Coleman request the pleasure of the company of (space to enter guest's names) on the occasion of the marriage of Tamryn Sandy and James Kirby ...

If you'd prefer less formal wording, speak to your stationery supplier as the space that's available on the card itself will put constraints on what you can say. They'll also be able to give you lots of ideas and sample wordings to choose from. If you are having an evening reception, you might also like to indicate when this may finish. The 'formal' way to word this would be to say 'Carriages at Midnight' but if you prefer something a little more relaxed, you could say 'Last Dance at Midnight'. Giving this information can be very helpful, particularly for older guests, those who have to travel some distance home or those who are booking babysitters!

Information Sheets

More and more couples are including an information sheet along with their invitations, but as this is a relatively new trend, how do you know what to include and is it necessary? A well-written information sheet can save you a lot of work in the long-run because it immediately gives all the relevant details to guests so no-one has to call you to find out about local accommodation or facilities available at your venue.

You can include any information that you feel is relevant to the day and to your guests but good things to include are:

* Directions to the venue or venues, the address, telephone number and even website details if appropriate.
* Details of local accommodation in case guests want to stay over and not journey home that night. If you can, include places covering most price brackets, as all your guests will have varying available funds.
* Phone numbers for local taxi firms. Do encourage guests to book their return journey early and this is especially important if you're in a more rural location.
* What facilities there are for elderly guests or families with young children (baby changing etc.).
* If your venue doesn't allow paper confetti, it's good to warn people not to bring any.
* You can ask guests with special dietary needs to let you know as soon as possible.
* Where people can park their cars (and if any payment is required).

* Any warnings i.e., lots of candles, a pond in the grounds, steep steps, etc.
* If you're having a cash bar, mention it here so people can bring enough cash for the evening.
* Details of local tourist sights in case any guests want to make a weekend of it.
* Remind people not to take pictures during the ceremony and to turn their mobile phones off.
* Some couples who are staying at a hotel with a number of their guests arrange to meet everyone for breakfast the following morning. If you're thinking about doing this, or even having a barbecue or picnic somewhere, it's good to put details on the information sheet.

Information sheets can take many forms – single sheets of paper or printed packs. You can write them as bullet points or in an A–Z format or you can even put all that information and more on your own wedding website. Websites can be built very easily and many of the major wedding information sites offer facilities for users to put together their own pages at a very low cost.

CHAPTER CHECKLIST

This chapter concentrated on dealing with most of the people who'll be with you to celebrate your wedding. Make sure you keep the following in mind:

✳ If you decide not to invite children, you need to be consistent and be prepared for a little backlash. This is something that can cause quite a wedding controversy so be happy in the choice that you've made.

✳ Disregard the convention that wedding invitations need only be sent six weeks in advance. Remember that lots of people have other commitments, especially around summer holidays or those with jobs that involve shift work so the more notice you can give, the better.

✳ Your RSVP date should be two or three weeks before the point at which you need to provide confirmed numbers to your venue or caterer (this also allows some time to chase anyone who has not replied!).

✳ An information sheet included with invitations can prevent you from having to answer the same questions over and over! Think about your plans and tell guests anything that might make things easier for them (but don't give away all your surprises for the day!).

Ten
The Gift List

The etiquette debate over including details of your wedding gift list with your invitation will never be resolved! Some people feel it saves time and others feel it's too rude to ask like this. If you don't want to include details, you could put a few lines on your information sheet or in with the invitations just letting guests know who to contact for details of the wedding list. If you do include them, most people don't mind at all. In fact, most guests are happy to have the information to hand. However, as with all things wedding related, you're bound to upset someone whatever you do. Just make sure you're happy with whatever decision you make.

Gift lists were originally started to help newlyweds furnish their first home together with basic items. Nowadays people still like to bring presents to weddings or to buy the happy couple something to 'set up home with'. However, gifts have now moved on to updating what couples already have, buying special items or even making charitable donations.

Organising Your Wedding List

There are a number of ways in which you can do this but try to pick a way that will suit most of your guests (for example, if most of them don't have internet access don't use a purely on-line company). Here's a run down of your options.

Do It Yourself

You can make your own list, either in a note-book that can be passed around so people can rip out the page with the details of the gift they'd like to buy, which avoids duplicates, or you could provide one person (e.g., a mum) with the list and people can call her for ideas, although you may end up with a few doubles this way! If you're technical, you could publish the list 'on-line' and let guests mark the items they'll buy. However you do it, you need to give exact information about the item, its price, a reference number if possible, where it can be purchased from and even delivery instructions.

Store Lists

Large high-street stores such as John Lewis, Debenhams and Marks and Spencer can hold your wedding list. You go into your chosen store, walk around and decide which items you would like on your list and they co-ordinate it. Details are held centrally on computer so guests can go into their local branch and make a purchase. You'll usually have one delivery of gifts before the wedding and another afterwards. Some stores offer a gift-wrapping service (often at a charge) and some will give you a percentage of the total amount spent on gifts from your list back as vouchers. This means you can often buy anything that wasn't chosen by guests. Before deciding on which store to use, check that the store you register with has plenty of things you'd like, find out what they charge guests for 'delivery' and what happens if there are any price increases or problems with product availability when your list is 'live'. Some also allow you to buy items left on your list when it closes for a discounted rate. If that's the case, putting a sofa or new television on your list isn't such a crazy idea after all!

Internet Gift Lists

A number of internet-based companies provide gift-list services. They basically take branded items and sell them on-line. You can choose from Alessi juicers to Ralph Lauren bedding. The disadvantage here is that the costs of the gifts are often higher and there can be problems for people without internet access as they have to call a customer service centre to make enquiries or purchases and they won't be able to see a picture of what they're buying. The advantage is that you can set the list up at midnight on a Sunday if that suits you and you often get a wider range of goods than from a high-street store.

How Much to Put on the List

Always put more items on the list than the number of people you're inviting. If a few people buy you more than one present, the list will run out before everyone has had a chance to make a purchase. Also, people like to have a choice and effectively 'surprise' you with their present. Most stores and on-line gift lists will allow you to mark the presents that are a high priority which increases the chance of you getting all the glasses or sheets that you ask for! If the list does start to run dry, you'll often be contacted to make some further choices.

When to Do It

It's not a good idea to choose your gift list too far in advance (however tempting this is!) in case of product range changes or price alterations. Most stores will let you register your interest in a list (and give you a list number) 12 months or so in advance but only invite you to pick your list four to six months before the big day. Your list will usually 'go live' and be open to purchases roughly six weeks before your wedding date. Don't worry if, when the list goes live, that it's a little slow. Most people wait until just before the wedding (or at least until the payday before!) to make a purchase.

THE GIFT LIST

How to Tell People

Etiquette says you shouldn't tell people about your list until after they've accepted your invitation although more and more people do include details of their gift list with the invitations. If you have a list at a store, they often provide you with little cards showing your list number and the 'live' date that you can enclose with the invitations. If you fancy something a little more personal, you can handwrite or print a little slip saying that 'presence is more important than presents' but if people would like to buy you a gift, your list is held at ... Alternatively, you can wait until you receive a 'yes' and then send out details of the gift list or just wait until you're asked!

What to Put on Your List

Once you've decided how to organise your list, you have to choose what goes on it and the answer to this is – whatever you would like! Make sure, however, there is a wide range of prices on the list as some people might like to buy you lots of little things, while others might be more generous than you imagine. Also, don't feel bad about including one or two very expensive items as friends and relations will often club together to buy you something that you'd really like. A good idea is to walk through your house before you set up your list and make a note of everything you'd like for each room then pick the exact item from a store or on-line.

If you've been together some time and the thought of another bundle of towels fills you with horror or if you'd just like to do something a little different, there are plenty of alternatives to the traditional home-based gift lists. One word of caution however – explain your plans properly to your guests as most of them will be expecting to buy you a conventional gift. Some of the smaller ideas can also be added to a traditional list if you'd like. So, what are your options?

Gift Vouchers

If you'd like to buy something special from one source, why not ask for gift vouchers? You could even let your guests know what it is you hope to purchase so they know what the vouchers will be used for (very handy if you're asking for high street vouchers so they don't think you're just going to buy more shoes!) A few stores, such as Selfridges, run an 'account' for couples where guests can basically pay money into your fund and then you're free to spend it in the store.

Food and Wine

You could start your wine cellar or treat yourself to some luxury goodies that you'd not normally buy. Some of the big wine retailers such as Berry Bros and Rudd can offer advice and help you with your list. Somewhere like Fortnum and Mason would be a wonderful place to pick yourself some gorgeous foodie treats. If you're a known gastronome, this could be brilliant.

Something Arty

If you'd like one fantastic piece of art to decorate your home then you could speak to the gallery concerned to see if they'd be able to help you with some form of gift voucher. If not, you could let everyone have the details of your intended purchase and open a special bank account for them to pay money into.

Honeymoon Heaven

If you'd like your guests to help fund a heavenly honeymoon, you could set up a honeymoon gift list with a company such as Trailfinders where your guests pay into your honeymoon account and their contributions are deducted from the total cost of your honeymoon. Or, you could work out roughly how much various elements of your honeymoon would cost so that guests can pay for you to have a champagne breakfast in bed or a snorkelling safari.

Savings

If you're maybe saving for a new house or a trip around the world, you could ask guests to buy you something like Premium Bonds which are a little 'easier' on guests than just asking for money.

Charitable Donations

This is the option for the truly selfless! Instead of any form of gift, you could ask guests to make donations to a specific charity. If you contact the charity you're thinking of helping, they'll be able to advise you on the best way to organise things – maybe cheques should be sent directly to them mentioning your names and they'll keep a record or cheques should be sent to someone in the wedding party who'll deal with writing out one large cheque. You can use a service such as The Alternative Gift List (see 'Further Information' at the back of this book) which lets your guests look at a number of charities and effectively 'buy' an item such as a water pump, a sight-restoring operation or food for an animal shelter.

Cash

Asking guests for money is still a big 'no no' for many people although the number of people asking for cash is rising. Be careful with this one, however, as it's likely to offend some people and you're bound to get a few who refuse to give money and will buy you something instead. It is still considered incredibly bad form to ask for money and effectively use this to fund your wedding as you're basically asking people to pay to attend. Plus you can't rely on the amounts guests might give to cover your costs anyway, so overall, it's a pretty risky idea. If you decide to ask for cash, think very carefully how you will do it – opening an invitation to find an enclosure simply saying 'we'd prefer cash to gifts' is a little mercenary. In this case, it might be prudent to wait until you're asked or just let word trickle out.

Gift Displays

A formal display of gifts is much less common than it was, mostly because stores often make deliveries after the wedding and because some people feel it puts pressure on the guests to spend more on gifts than they can maybe afford in case anyone sees their present and thinks they've been a little mean. However, if you do want to display your presents at your venue, you should arrange them carefully, grouping together items that go together (i.e., all kitchen items in one spot) but any duplicates should be placed a little way apart to try and avoid any embarrassment. If your presents consist of cheques or vouchers, you should not display the actual paper, but write a little note stating 'Voucher/Cheque from Mr and Mrs ...'.

Buying from the List

If a couple has gone to the trouble of setting up a gift list, it is good manners to use it and buy something that's actually wanted. However, there will always be some people who refuse to do this for whatever reason. How you handle this is up to you but just be polite – if you really don't want anything other than items from your list say something along the lines of 'I'm sorry Auntie Beryl but apart from the items on our list, there's nothing we'd like' – which might win them around. If not, be prepared to grin and bear it when the gift does arrive. You can't please all of the people all of the time!

Returning Gifts

This really isn't a good idea. Even if you do end up with a gift that you don't want, someone has gone to the time and trouble to buy it for you so returning it for store credit is a little mean. However, if it's a duplicate item, making a swap is okay.

If you're heading straight off on honeymoon, delegate someone to collect all the cards and gifts from the venue and take them home for you to pick up on your return.

Gifts Brought to the Wedding

Even if you've got a list at a store that will deliver presents to you, a number of guests still prefer to bring their gift with them. Do make sure there's somewhere safe for them to be stored and, if you've asked for vouchers, ensure that unopened cards are also locked carefully away until you can be sure of the contents.

CHAPTER CHECKLIST

You might think that setting up your gift list is one of the nicest parts of organising your wedding but even this can be a minefield. Hopefully, this chapter will see you through with a smile! Remember to keep the following in mind:

✳ Be very careful when putting your guest list together. Try to find something that will make it easy for all your guests to buy from.

✳ There are plenty of alternatives to the traditional gift list if you don't want towels or photo frames, so look around before you make a final decision.

✳ Etiquette says details of the gift list should not be included with the invitations, but this has been changed recently and more couples are choosing to ignore this advice. Do what you are comfortable with.

✳ If you are having a high-street list, register with a store sooner rather than later – most only take a limited number of lists so make sure you do not miss out.

Eleven
Entertainment

Everyone loves a good party, especially at a wedding, but this is where it can get expensive. In this chapter, we'll look at areas in which money is well spent and plenty of alternatives for 'non-dancing' entertainment if you really don't want to be on the dance floor all night. There will also be lots of suggestions for fun ways that you can involve your guests and also plenty of smaller ideas that will have a big impact. Ultimately, wedding entertainment isn't simply a question of booking the most expensive band, it's about putting together a package that will involve as many guests as possible because that's what generates the fabulous atmosphere that people remember. As great as a DJ might be, if you and your guests aren't likely to pack the dance floor, it will have been a waste of your money. Plus, I've not forgotten the smaller guests, because they need entertaining too!

Music

Musical entertainment is always really popular at weddings and with good reason. It makes you feel good, it can be romantic, emotional or just plain funny and there are lots of ways that you can include it in your day. Well chosen music can make an event feel more welcoming to guests and it actually encourages conversation to flow because people don't feel that their voices are standing out so much in the silence. Take some time to really think about your musical choices, they should reflect your personalities and mean something to you both. If you're really not into classical music, there's no reason to include it and contemporary pieces can work just as well. Likewise, the song that you choose for your first dance will stick in your memory for the rest of your life so choose wisely!

Live Music

This is fantastic but it's often more expensive than a DJ. For your evening reception, you can hire cover bands, jazz or swing ensembles, 60s groups, or those that play anything and everything you ask. There are listings of bands in wedding magazines, the Yellow Pages and local publications but getting a personal recommendation is always good. Another alternative is to source your band through a booking agency who'll send you demo CDs and deal with all the paperwork for you. Bands will usually play 'sets' consisting of 30–50 minutes and then take a break before resuming. You should check what happens during the breaks – some bands will provide CDs to play but others don't and you'll probably want people to continue partying! Most bands require a deposit payment with the remainder to be paid to them on the day but this is something to check in their terms and conditions when you book. A band often require more space than a DJ so you will need to think about this before you book too. You also need to check with your venue that they allow live music.

Some couples also decide to go for live music during their ceremony or drinks reception. Again, this does make the event feel very luxurious but if this wasn't listed as one of your priorities when you did your early brainstorming, don't feel it's something you must have. A suitable CD is just as good for background music here and it would be wiser to put more of your available budget into the music for the evening reception when it's more of a feature.

As I've mentioned before, you need to consider the space available to you. Musicians and all their equipment can take up quite a bit of room so be sure that there's plenty for them to play in. Speak to your venue and see what they recommend, does live music tend to work well? Remember also that live music is something to watch as well as something to listen to. Ideally one large room is best as opposed to smaller interconnecting rooms.

If you decide to book some musicians for your wedding, there are a few things to make sure you check before you sign on the dotted line:

* Exactly how long will they play for?
* How long will each set be?
* How many breaks will they take and what will happen during these? Will they play CDs for example?
* How flexible are they in the music that they play?
* Do you have to feed them? Contracts for some bands state that they must have a hot meal before they start to play whilst others just ask for sandwiches. Make sure you know what's expected and ensure that you're happy with the extra cost that might involve.
* Will they need a dedicated room to change in or store some equipment? If so, speak with your venue to ensure that this will be available for them.
* When will they set up and how long will that take? If you've got a limited amount of time available during the 'turn around' of a room from dinner to evening, will they be able to set up, sound check and be ready to play when you'd like?
* Have they worked at your venue before? Again, there's no 'correct' answer to that question but it's often quite reassuring if they know where they're going on the day!

DJ

DJs are often cheaper than live musicians and can create just as much atmosphere with the right choice of music. You should liaise with your DJ before the big day and provide him with a playlist – songs you want to hear and even songs you definitely don't want! They should also bring their own sound system and even lights, but if you've got older guests, make sure the volume isn't too loud. Some venues have noise-limiting systems where the power is automatically shut off if the volume goes above a certain level. If there are any restrictions like this in place at your venue, do make sure your DJ is aware of them.

The questions aimed at live musicians also apply to DJs but do be certain that they've got the exact track for your first dance. If you've chosen a particular version of a particular song, be very clear to them which one it is so that you get exactly what you want on the night.

TAMRYN'S TIP

Since DJs usually require less space than a band, they can quite often set up before your meal so there's no rush to get ready in the 'turn around' period. And for a little extra cash, they'll often provide background music during dinner as well.

The First Dance and More

Of course, the main focus of musical entertainment is 'the first dance', the mere mention of which is usually enough to throw the groom into a panic! You can choose anything for a first dance but most couples pick something that has a certain meaning for them or a song with particularly appropriate words (if you had to omit a song from your civil ceremony because it contained 'religious' words, now would be a perfect time to use it). The first dance is usually announced by the band or DJ and is taken as the 'official' start of an evening reception – guests are very unlikely to dance before this point so don't wait too long.

Some couples go to dancing lessons or buy videos to teach themselves how to waltz or tango but there are plenty that just shuffle around gazing lovingly at each other! If you really don't want to be dancing for long on your own, find a few friendly couples beforehand and ask them to join you on the floor after the first chorus.

It's 'traditional' for there to be a second dance which is usually the bride with her father. This can be a really touching moment and other couples often join in at this point too. The groom can dance with his mother, the bride's mother can dance with the groom's father and the best man should ask the chief bridesmaid. Try to pick a song that will entice as many people onto the dance floor as possible, so speak to your band or DJ and ask them for some suitable suggestions.

Another enjoyable moment can be 'the last dance' and this can be great fun as all your guests pile on to the dance floor to give you a great send-off. This dance is usually a 'communal' dance with everyone linking arms or forming a circle around the newlyweds and it can often get quite emotional. Some favourite pieces for this dance are 'New York, New York', 'I've had the time of my life', 'You'll never walk alone' or 'Bring me Sunshine'. Again, if you're not sure what to pick, speak to the experts!

Fun and Games

It's great to to have some fun with your nearest and dearest at your wedding and there are plenty of options available to suit all budgets. But, before you get completely carried away and fill every minute with entertainments, remember that guests want to have some time to relax and enjoy the day – they don't want to spend it being marched from one activity to another! Think carefully about when you'll want to provide entertainment – the most popular times to 'fill' are the gaps between the ceremony and dinner and the dinner and dancing. You might like to think about table games for dinner, particularly if you're seating guests with people they might not already know, as a well-planned activity breaks the ice and gets people talking. Here are some suggestions and there's something below for all budgets.

Casinos

Organising a casino is a brilliant way to have some fun if you don't want to be dancing. Although they're reasonably expensive, the price is comparable with musical entertainment for a large number of tables and obviously less if you just want one table to run alongside a DJ. Companies bring everything they need with them from chips and croupiers to fun money and dice. Blackjack and roulette are always the most popular but there are other games available if you're booking a larger number of tables.

Fireworks

Obviously, a professionally organised display that lasts some time is going to be quite expensive but you can arrange shorter displays for a reasonable cost. If entertainment was high on your priority list, fireworks can certainly give your evening a big bang! You need to be sure that your venue allows them, however, before you arrange anything. A cheaper alternative would be to provide everyone with long-length sparklers to accompany the last dance. If you choose this option do keep in mind some common-sense safety precautions.

Caricaturists/Silhouette Artists

These can be great fun, though they are at the top end of the price scale. The artist wanders around groups of guests, drawing or snipping as they go and then the guest is given the finished creation as a brilliant keepsake memento of the day.

Magicians

Again, one of the more expensive options, but a close-up magician can help make your day, well, magical! They can entertain small groups of guests at a time and can be a real talking point. As the magician obviously needs to be able to talk to the people they're entertaining, they work best during drinks receptions or 'turn around' periods when the music is low or non-existent rather than during the evening when the volume is set more loudly!

Chocolate Fountains

Part entertainment and part catering attraction, chocolate fountains have become very popular recently. However, you have to consider the number of guests that you have because cramming a hundred people around one fountain isn't very practical. Also, if you've got a lot of children, you need to have a pretty blasé attitude to mess and the prospect of your gorgeous dress being smeared with chocolate. They're not as expensive as they once were but double-check how much chocolate and fruit items for dipping are included in the package.

Balloon Races

These can be a great focal point and they also make great photographs! In the 'middle' range of expense, each guest is given a helium-filled balloon with a tag tied on giving the details of the balloon's launch site and date and then all are released at the same time. It can take a bit of co-ordinating to get the balloons all going up at the same time but it's certainly fun. There are rules and regulations you must follow, however, if you're considering a balloon release. These can be found on

The Balloon Association's website (details can be found in the 'Further Information' section of this book).

Quizzes

These can be great fun and are free to organise! You just need to spend a little bit of time thinking up the questions and you're ready to go. It's a good idea to ask the guests questions about you both – where you met, who asked who out first, where you went on your first date and the like. Giving options for the answers can make 'marking' easier and it makes completing the quiz simpler for guests too. Place the quiz sheets on the tables during dinner with a note asking each table to complete them before dessert. The best man and bridesmaid can then 'mark' them and the winning table could be announced during the speeches. If you want to give a prize, a bottle of something to the winners will always go down very well! Of course, if you've not got the time or the inclination to write a quiz, you can buy ready-written boxes of 'table trivia' which you could leave in lounge areas or on outside tables during drinks or the 'turn around' period.

Child-sized Entertainment

If you're inviting children to your wedding, it can be a good idea to consider their needs when you're planning the entertainment. They're probably not going to want to sit and listen to the speeches or hang around while photos are being taken and the adults are sipping their drinks so taking some time to plan a few activities for them will make the day much more enjoyable (and more peaceful!) for everyone. Again, there's child-sized entertainment to fit every budget. Remember that sometimes with children, the simpler the activity, the better!

Professional Help

Hiring a couple of nursery nurses might be the more expensive option, but it can also be the easiest, particularly if you've got a lot of children attending and you're sure you want an 'adults only' dinner. There are agencies that specialise in providing qualified, vetted staff for events or you could approach a nursery that's close to the venue. Most professionals will arrive with games and activities for the children and will also oversee their own tea party.

The Entertainer

Booking an entertainer for a shorter period of time can be cheaper and just as much fun. Perhaps a balloon modeller, a face painter or a magician would work well?

Treasure Hunts

If the children aren't going to be needed for photos (and let's face it, getting them to all stand still and face the right way at the right moment takes some doing!), how about organising a little treasure hunt to fill the time? You need to be a bit prepared and write the clues in advance but that's about it! Put a prize or goody bags at the end of the trail and these can then be used to keep the little ones entertained over dinner.

Goody Bags

Making up goody bags for children is becoming more and more popular and with good reason – it's a great way to keep them occupied, amused and quiet during dinner and the speeches! You can buy these ready-made from companies that specialise in putting together surprise parcels for children or you can spend a bit more time and a bit less money and buy everything yourself. Obviously, including things that can be done quietly is the best idea – there's no point including noisy games or musical instruments and then expect them not to be used! Paper, pencils and crayons for the younger ones and mini-building kits or jewellery-making packs for older children work really well. I'd suggest you don't include sweets in these packs, particularly if you've paid for children's meals!

Kids' Drawings

Keeping the children occupied during dinner is always a big worry so give them paper and pencils and ask them to draw a picture of the wedding. Give a little prize to all entrants and keep their drawings – there's bound to be some budding Monets in the group and getting a little person's perspective on the day is always interesting!

Video Party

If your venue is able to set aside a room for children, set some videos or DVDs running and give them some space where they can get away from everything and crash out. Children can often get quite 'hyper' at weddings because there's so much going on. Giving them a place where they can have some 'quiet time' is a good idea.

Craft Area

Setting up some tables with craft activities works really well – the children can have fun and get creative at the same time. They usually end up with things to take home although you'll be surprised at how many of these items are then given to the newlyweds which is quite a touching gesture.

Involving Guests

The secret to successful entertainment is to try and get your guests as involved as possible and there are lots of ways to do this. Again, don't feel that you need to use all of these ideas. Pick the ones that appeal to you the most and the ones that will suit the style of your day the best.

Play DJ

Get everyone on the dance floor by letting them decide what gets played! Include a line on your invitations or on your RSVP card asking for their favourite song. Then compile a list and hand it over to your DJ (including names if you want 'dedications'). It's best to do this in advance so that you can be sure your DJ has the music requested.

Video Diary

If you're having a videographer, ask them if they can set up a video diary room. All your guests can leave you a personal message that's included at the end of your video. You'll get some hilarious and heartwarming messages from guests. Just be sure you let everyone know where the room is!

Photoboard

People always like to look at photos so photoboards are a fabulous conversation piece. Photos of you both growing up are brilliant (especially if there are some 'trendy at the time' hairstyles included!), as are pics of you on various holidays or nights out together. For a twist, collect baby photos of every guest or just the wedding party. Put them all on a huge piece of card and display them at your venue.

Ceremony Promise

Including your guests in the ceremony will make them feel extra special. Speak to your officiant and see if you can include a line where the guests promise to support the bride and groom in the future. The guests can all answer 'we will' and it will show them just how important they are to you both.

Speech Sweepstake

Ask all guests to guess the length of the best man's speech. Everyone can pay 50p and the winner gets to choose a charity to donate it to, or you can forget the fee and just give a bottle of champagne to the closest guess. You'll need someone to note the guesses and, of course, delegate someone responsible to time it (most mobile phones have stopwatch facilities on them so no extra equipment is required).

Table Cameras

Table cameras are incredibly popular and with good reason. Just leave one or two on each reception table and let guests play paparazzi. To make sure you get the best shots possible, make sure they know to use the flash and wind them on! Also, when the room is changed round for your evening party, make sure the cameras are still left out. Delegate someone to collect finished cameras or make sure your venue saves them.

Poetic Moments

Let those creative juices flow! Ask each table to create a little wedding poem or provide them with the start of a limerick. Collect them up before the speeches, let the best man vet them (always a good idea!) and then he can read out the best ones before his toast. You can keep them all and add them to your keepsake box.

Table Toasts

Get everyone involved in the speeches and use up all that toast champagne! Ask each table to compose a toast and get one person from each table to make a toast. Your best man, toastmaster or co-ordinator can help people and introduce each table so that guests get to express their feelings for you both. Give guidelines so the toasts are kept short and sweet!

Taking Table Centres

It's a shame to waste those gorgeous table centres so how about letting one guest from each table take one home with them? It could be someone who's helped you during the planning, someone who's travelled a long way or just someone who deserves a little gift. Mark their place cards in some way or break the good news during the introductions.

Photos to Go

Some photographers can set up a mini studio at your venue and each guest, couple or family can have a photo taken. The photo is then printed immediately and can be taken away at the end of the night. Everyone gets a brilliant keepsake and they can always look back at the photo and think of you both.

Sparkly Exit

This is a brilliant idea that gives both of you a wonderful send-off at the end of the night. Give your guests one or two decent-length sparklers, line them up outside and then you can run through a path of sparklers to your car before you drive off into the sunset! This does take some organising, however, and you will need to designate a few people with the responsibility of lighting everyone's sparklers once everyone is lined up. Long-length sparklers will last anything up to four minutes but make sure there is somewhere suitable for them to be disposed of. Sparklers can be dangerous so people should wear gloves if possible and children should be supervised at all times.

Candlelight Ceremony

This is a great touch for winter weddings. Get your ushers to hand everyone entering the ceremony room a candle then make your vows by candlelight. It's incredibly atmospheric and ever so romantic. But do remember the safety rules.

Communal Food

Get everyone talking over dinner. If you can arrange food to share as opposed to individual plates, people get chatting instantly. Think of a big plate of anti-pasti or even a chocolate fondue for dessert.

Late Cake

Cutting your cake later is a fabulous way of involving your guests in the action. Make it the formal start of your evening reception so everyone can get a look at your gorgeous cake

ENTERTAINMENT

before it's sliced up. While you have everyone's attention, go straight onto the dance floor so there's no break in the action and dip in atmosphere.

Speech Surprises

Surprises during the speeches are always good as guests get to feel they're part of a joke or special moment as they share the surprise with everyone else. Humorous photos tacked under chairs that are found at the right moment or a special gift delivered to a happy recipient brings all the guests into the action.

Big Welcome

Make a really big entrance into dinner and get everyone on their feet. Delegate someone to get your guests seated while the bride and groom wait outside, in order to give out all the information about guestbooks, cameras, etc., before asking the guests to stand and give the bride and groom a huge welcome. There will be loads of clapping, cheering, whistling and camera flashes! The bride and groom get a huge welcome and all the guests enjoy 'making some noise'!

Popping Champagne

Get some guest participation into your speeches! If you are speaking, give some trusted individuals a bottle of un-popped champagne with a cue from your speech and get them to pop the cork at the pre-ordained time.

As you can see, there are plenty of touches that you can add to the day that needn't be expensive but they'll all make the day more enjoyable for everyone. Guests will really appreciate these little touches and you'll both get a big kick from seeing everyone so happy.

CHAPTER CHECKLIST

From this chapter, it's clear to see that the only limits to entertainment are your budget and your imagination. Don't be scared to throw in a few unexpected twists or activities but be careful that you don't try to fill every minute of the day – people do want time to sit and talk and just enjoy the wedding.

❋ Remember that live music is often more expensive than a DJ so look again at your priority list and your budget.

❋ Check carefully through any contracts and ask lots of questions before you commit to booking.

❋ You might want to think about including some other entertainment and this can be anything from a casino to a short quiz for guests. Just remember that whatever you choose, it should be something that will include as many people as possible.

❋ Take some time to consider the children that will be attending and remember that any child is likely to get bored at what is mainly an adult event. Try to give them something to do, even if it's just a pile of paper and some crayons.

❋ Think about various ways to include your guests in the day because that is guaranteed to get everyone raving about your day. You'll love seeing everyone so happy and they'll love you for being so thoughtful.

Twelve
Memories …

Ask any newly married couple about their wedding and most will say how quickly the day flies by which is a shame in some ways because I'm sure everyone wants to prolong the day as much as possible. Every couple wants to be able to remember their wedding and modern photography and videography packages can be brilliant but quite a strain on the budget. I hope that this chapter will help you look at what you want from these two items and how to ensure that you get it. We'll also look at lots of other ways in which the day can be remembered.

Photographs

For the majority of couples, photography will always feature highly on their list of priorities and with good reason. Being able to look back at images that have really captured the spirit of the day is one of the best lasting memories that you can have of your day. I would suggest that this is one area in which you spend as much as you can afford because whilst flowers and favours are nice to have, they're only with you for one day whereas your wedding album will be with you for the rest of your life.

As we'll see in Chapter 15, there are plenty of things to keep in mind when meeting and choosing suppliers and, of course, lots of those pointers apply to photographers as well.

In this section, however, I'm going to give you information that's specific to packages and services that you'll need to know about so that you're armed with all the necessary knowledge before you start hunting for your perfect picture taker.

Essentially, there are three main styles of wedding photography:

* Traditional photography involves a number of posed group shots being taken, mainly in colour. There are no spontaneous shots or photos of the small details of the day in traditional albums.
* Reportage is a very popular word and means that all photos are taken spontaneously with absolutely no set up shots. If you want a real storybook of your day, this would be great but you might miss out on a few group shots.
* Contemporary albums contain a mixture of posed and unposed photos in a mix of colour and black and white.

Look at some wedding magazines to find the types of images that you like and then do your research to find some photographers that can provide the style that you're searching for. Of course, one of the first things to check is that they're within your budget, so what should you expect to pay? This does depend on the style (traditional albums cost less than reportage and contemporary packages), but also what you get for what you're paying. Don't just look at the final figure, but take the following into account as well:

* How many images will you actually get? Are you given a lot but then have to choose a limited number from that selection for your album and pay for any additional prints that you want or will you get a copy of every photo?

* Will an album be included in the price? If not, are you happy to source your own and put it together?
* How many hours will the photographer be with you? Will they cover every part of the day that is important to you?
* Will you be given the negatives or can you buy them for an extra cost? If you think you're going to be ordering lots of reprints, this could save you money.
* How much are reprints and what sizes are offered?
* Are there any 'hidden' costs in the package? Does the photographer request that a meal is provided for them or will there be additional mileage charges to your venue?

Knowing the answers to these questions will allow you to compare the packages and prices of various photographers easily. You may find that what initially looks like a great deal isn't so appealing when you've added in some additional costs.

Briefing Your Photographer

Once you've used these pointers and you are sure you've asked all the questions from Chapter 15, you'll be able to book your wedding photographer (and that's a big tick on the 'to do' list!). You'll need to meet with your photographer before the day to talk through everything so be sure to let them know the following:

* When and where you'll be getting ready on the day if your package includes the preparations of the bride and groom.
* Times that you've planned for the ceremony, posed photographs, dinner and dancing.
* Anything that they should specifically be aware of, for example, features at the venue or family situations.

* Details of photographs that you really want taken. Most photographers will give you a list of photos and you can simply tick the ones that you'd like (bride and groom with bride's grandparents or groom with the rugby club lads) but do point out any photos that are really important to you. Don't feel that you need to list everything because if you're comfortable with your photographer, you should trust them to take the 'major' shots without having to be prompted. If you want to go armed with an absolutely exhaustive list, there are plenty of examples on-line and in magazines.
* Let them know when you'll be back from honeymoon as most photographers will be able to have some proofs ready for you to view on your return (which is really nice to look forward to!).

On the day itself, I can promise you that however self-conscious you think you'll feel about having endless photos taken, it won't be as bad as you imagine at all! Try to relax and enjoy being the centre of attention and if you're feeling ecstatic, let it come through in your photos. It's true that a happy, relaxed bride who's enjoying herself will always look great in photos, so laugh, smile and love every minute of the day and you're going to be surprised at how great you look.

Videos

Wedding videos are something that you either love or hate. Whilst quite a few couples know that they want a video, they don't rate it as being as important as their wedding photos.

As with photography, you need to know exactly what you'll be getting for your money before you sign on the dotted line and these are some things to check:

* How many hours will they shoot and how long will the edited video be?

✳ Will they require people to wear microphones during the speeches?

✳ Is an additional light going to be required for the first dance? If so, are you happy with the spotlight being on you at this time?

✳ How many copies of the finished product will you receive and will they be on video or DVD?

You'll also need to ask whoever is performing your ceremony if there's an additional charge for taking a video.

Amateur Videos

Of course, quite a few people want a record of the day but haven't placed a video high enough up their list of priorities to spend a fortune on it so quite a few couples ask friends or relatives with video cameras to become movie makers and record key moments. If you do this, remember these tips:

✳ Be sure to tell them exactly what you'd like recorded, for example, speeches, ceremony, first dance, cake cutting.

✳ Try to choose someone who isn't closely involved with the main wedding party otherwise they'll be having to do two jobs on the day!

✳ Remember that you're not going to get a professional-looking end product (unless of course the person you choose happens to be a camera man!) so don't expect amazing results.

✳ Try to give them plenty of warning for important moments because it might take them longer to get set up than it would a professional.

Ultimately, wedding videos can be fun to look back on but they don't tend to have the same timeless appeal as photographs. If you've got a figure in mind that has to cover both photography and videography packages, I'd suggest you spend a larger proportion of that money on your photos.

Guest Books

Another brilliant way to remember your day is through the eyes of your closest friends and family. Guest books are essentially an opportunity for your nearest and dearest to record their thoughts and feelings about the day and to wish you well for your futures together. Whilst a book is one of the most popular ways to involve guests and gather their thoughts on the event, there are plenty of other options too:

* A signing plate is great, especially if you're both food lovers or keen cooks. Guests sign an unglazed plate with a special pen and then the piece is glazed and fired and returned to you ready for culinary use. More expensive than a simple guest book but it might be likely to get more use.

* If you speak to your photographer before the day, they might be able to provide you with a photographic mount that all the guests can sign. This can then be used to frame a large-size reprint of your favourite wedding photos to be hung somewhere suitable in your home. This is a great option, particularly if you were going to order a print to display in your house anyway, as this just makes it a bit more special.

* Including photos in guest books is a great way to spice them up although it takes a bit more work. Someone needs to take Polaroid photos of all the guests and stick them into the book before it's passed around to be signed. Each couple then writes their message on the page with their image. Lots of fun but you need to be a bit organised here to ensure that there are photos and messages from everyone to avoid ugly blank pages.

* Make-a-Wish cards are another thoughtful idea. Each guest simply writes their wish for you both on a small card and pops it into a bowl or other container. These cards can then be included in your wedding album or keepsake box. This is no more expensive than a standard guest book but there's more of a chance the wishes will be read again if they're included with your photos.

TAMRYN'S TIP

It's a shame when guest books (or alternatives) aren't completed by all the guests so either make an announcement as to the whereabouts of the book or delegate a bridesmaid or usher with the task of circulating the book amongst the guests and encouraging them to write in it for you.

Absent Loved Ones

Of course, weddings can be emotional events and they can be even more emotional when people can't be there to share the day with you. More and more couples are looking for ways to remember loved ones on their wedding day whilst not dampening the mood of the party. There are plenty of ways to do this and here are a few suggestions that might help you:

* Don't feel that you can't mention a loved one in a speech. A few words mentioning how much they would have enjoyed the day or laughed at a certain part of it is a very gentle way of doing this. Please don't worry if you get emotional either – weddings are emotional occasions and absolutely everyone will totally understand why you are feeling that way.

* Photographs can work really well, and it's even nicer if you can use photographs of loved ones on their wedding days too. Perhaps stand them next to the cake so the image is there for people to see without you having to say something if you'd prefer not to.

* Menus and the order of ceremony have usually got some spare space somewhere so why not include a few words about loved ones here? You can say what you like in a very understated way that isn't terribly obvious, which works very well if you'd prefer to keep things low key.

* Forgo your favours and instead consider making a donation to a charity that has some relevance to your loved one. You could put a little note on the menus, on the backs of place cards or even make a little reference to this in your speech.

* Music, of course, can be incredibly meaningful so you could select a suitable piece to accompany the signing of the register or even as your first dance song. It might not be obvious to everyone why you have chosen that tune, but if you know the meaning behind it, that's all that matters.

* A large number of brides decide not to throw their bouquets at the end of the evening and instead arrange for it to be put on a gravestone or other memorial. This can be an opportunity for you to take some time out and have a few moments alone with your thoughts.

CHAPTER CHECKLIST

This chapter should have given you a good overview on how you can remember your wedding for years to come and how to remember others on the day itself. Both should be priorities and how you decide to do each is up to you but I'd like you to remember the following:

* Money spent on photography is never money wasted because the images will stay with you forever and it's through these that you'll be able to keep your memories of the day alive.

* Check and double-check exactly what is included in your photography package before you book and make sure that the photographer you choose produces the type of images that you like.

* Videos are fun to watch but if you've not got room in the budget to hire a professional, you can get a very basic record of the day from a friend with a video camera.

* Getting comments from guests is a great way to get an alternative view of the day and you don't have to confine yourself to the standard 'guest book' if you don't want to.

* Remember absent loved ones at your wedding if the people involved were important to you. Take some time to think about how you would like to remember them and what you are most comfortable with.

Thirteen
Dressing Up and Looking Good

There's no doubt about it that on your wedding day, all eyes will be on you! It's your day in the spotlight so it's understandable that most brides want to look their absolute best. The wedding dress is a major part of the transformation from 'every day' to 'special day' as are the accessories and make-up, so this chapter covers everything that you need to know about dressing up and looking good. There's also information for the guys in here too so leave the page open if you want to drop a few subtle hints!

Everyone looks forward to going dress shopping. However, quite a few brides-to-be find their experiences while searching for the perfect dress slightly demoralising. If you arm yourself with a few facts before you go, you'll know what to expect.

Dress Shops

The source of many a bridal complaint! Sometimes staff can be a little unhelpful and unwelcoming – if this happens to you, turn around and walk straight out. That particular shop might stock your favourite designer but so will lots of other places. You're going to be spending quite a sum so make sure you're treated well and the whole experience will be a lot more enjoyable. It's a good idea to call your dress shop in advance to make an appointment because this will ensure you get the attention you deserve and the time you need to make an informed choice. Weekends are notoriously busy in bridal shops. If you can manage it, a weekday visit is much better as you'll have more time and much more attention.

When you arrive, you'll probably be asked to look around the shop and decide on ten or so dresses you'd like to try on first. Don't panic if there's nothing in your size – the majority of shops only hold one size of each dress but they can either pin in a dress that's too big or hold a dress that's too small so you can see how it looks. This does annoy some people but unfortunately it is standard practice. The shop should also provide you with some shoes to try on when you're wearing each dress as it's helpful to see how easy it is to walk in a gown. Then, it's a matter of trying on gorgeous designs until you find 'the one'.

Here are some more tips to get the most out of your visit to the dress shop:

* Don't get disheartened if the dress you've been drooling over in magazines doesn't suit you. Ask the assistant to pick out something that they think would suit your shape.
* Choose dresses that show off your good points or hide your bad ones (see our guide below!)
* Gowns vary in price hugely so if you have an absolute maximum that you're willing to spend, don't try on dresses above this mark. Ask an assistant to guide you to designers who will fit your price range.
* Take someone whose opinion you really trust and who won't get bored watching you parade around. This isn't a decision that can, or should, be rushed.
* Don't feel pressured into ordering a dress. You can easily come back to place an order another day, but if you order before you're completely sure, cancelling can be expensive.
* Unless you're hugely body confident, wear 'Bridget Jones' style underwear because the assistant will

probably come into the changing room to help you into dresses.

* Wearing a strapless bra is also a good idea if you have one.
* Maybe take a bottle of water as the fitting rooms can sometimes get very hot.
* Try on various styles, even ones you don't think will suit you and don't be governed by how the dress looks on the hanger. Some gowns look drab and boring when they are hung up but absolutely wonderful once they are on.
* Don't expect to be allowed to take a photograph of a dress before you've ordered – the shops won't allow it in case you go elsewhere and have a copy made.
* If you find 'the one', try on a combination of shoes, tiaras, veils and all the other accessories, so you can decide what you would like and what will suit.

TAMRYN'S TIP

Do take a note of the names of designers or dress styles that you like so that you can find images on-line later or just so you can keep a track of what you've tried on and liked (particularly if you're visiting more than one boutique).

Ordering Your Dress

Once you have decided on your dress, the shop will place your order with the designer so you will need to pay the shop a deposit (usually 50 per cent of the cost of the dress) with the remainder to be paid when it arrives at the store and before any alterations. If you are planning on losing weight, order a dress that fits you NOW. It's easy to take a dress in, it's almost impossible to let it out if you don't make your target weight. The majority of stores include a caveat in their terms and conditions stating that you'll still have to buy the dress even if you can't get into it and you don't need the added pressure of having to diet in the run-up to your wedding. Dresses usually take between 3–6 months to order so give yourself plenty of time because last-minute panics over whether the dress will arrive aren't fun. Start looking roughly 12 months in advance but plenty of people order earlier than that. There are new collections of designs every year but styles don't tend to change that much.

TAMRYN'S TIP

Bridal gown sales often take place in the New Year before the new collections arrive at the shops so you can bag yourself a bargain here. Look in the national wedding magazines or local press for details of sale dates.

Alterations

Hardly anyone is a perfect size – most people are a few inches larger or smaller in various places so having your dress altered will turn it into a perfectly flattering fit. Alterations can be done from any point after your dress arrives at the shop but having them done too early, especially if you're losing weight, might not be a good idea. You will need to take your wedding shoes and underwear to your fitting so that the seamstress can get hem lengths and bodice tucks exactly right. At the first fitting, the dress will be 'pinned'. Seams will then be unpicked and resewn before your second fitting which is to check the alterations are perfect. If everything is okay, you will either be asked to take the dress home or you will be able to leave it with the shop until closer to the wedding. It's hard to set a budget for alterations but, as an estimate, it can be 10–15 per cent of the cost of the dress.

When you Get your Dress Home

Take it out of the bag and hang it up so that nothing is creased against the floor (this is important – but also difficult – if your gown has a train). If you need to cover your dress to protect it, an old duvet cover is better than a plastic bag as it lets the fabric breath. If you get creases in your dress, hang it in the bathroom and have a hot shower and the steam should help the creases to drop out. Ironing your dress isn't recommended because of all the layers and netting but if you must, lay a clean tea towel over the fabric so there's no chance of the iron marking your gorgeous gown. Try and avoid continually trying your dress on as the more you handle it, the more likely it is that it will get dirty or damaged and that's not what you need at all.

Styles to Suit all Shapes

Everyone looks good in different styles so here is a quick guide to help you:

* ✳ Empire line dresses will make a petite figure appear taller. They'll accentuate and flatter your curves.
* ✳ A-line strapless gowns will look great if you've got a slim upper body but as they flare out below the waist, they'll hide problem areas like bums and thighs.
* ✳ Backless dresses are for the daring amongst you with toned, smooth backs. Not for the faint-hearted as this is what people will see most during the ceremony.
* ✳ Off-the-shoulder designs will accentuate upper arms.

* Fabric that is layered and draped over the bodice will enhance a small bust.
* Halter-neck dresses look fab on brides with sexy shoulders.
* V-necked gowns are for brides who want to show off a perfect cleavage.
* If your legs are your best asset, why not go for a dress with a slit – go as high as you dare!

Shoes

Whether you choose traditional fabric bridal shoes, something more modern such as sandals, or even if you just use this opportunity to finally buy a pair of Jimmy Choo or Gina heels, have them by your first fitting so that if your dress needs to be taken up, it can be altered to the perfect length.

TAMRYN'S TIP

To help protect your feet against the pain caused by wearing heels, you might want to try the little pads that stick into your shoes to cushion the balls of your feet or heels. Look for a make such as 'TipToes' that stick to the inside of the shoe for maximum comfort but make sure you still have room to fit in the shoe!

Obviously you'll be spending the whole day standing, dancing and generally on your feet, so your shoes must be comfortable. Breaking them in around the house before the big day is a must. Wearing an old pair of socks over the top will stop the shoes getting mucky. Try rubbing the bottom of the shoes with sandpaper as this will help you to stop slipping on carpet. There are no rules with shoes – some people wear knee-high boots, others wear bridal trainers and some wear brightly coloured shoes that match their colour scheme. Another option is to have 'proper' shoes for the ceremony and dinner and something more practical, such as ballet shoes, for the dancing.

Tiaras

You can really be a princess for a day with a trendy tiara. There are all sorts to choose from – crowns, tiaras, jewelled Alice bands and elaborate head-dresses. It's good to try on a few tiaras when you try on dresses so that you know the basics – silver or gold, large or small, coloured or plain. Also, don't think that you need long hair or an elaborate 'up do' to wear a tiara, that's a myth – they suit all hair styles. If you can't find one that's 'you' in the stores, you could consider having one designed and made especially for you (an excellent option if you're having a 'theme' or want something unique). This isn't as expensive as it sounds and you can get good-quality personally designed tiaras for under £50.

Other Head-dresses

If you don't fancy a tiara but want something in your hair, there are plenty of other options:

* Flowers always look beautifully bridal. You could have one or two blooms tucked into your hair or go for it with a floral circlet. You'll need long-lasting flowers so they don't wilt before the end of the evening or you could go for silk flowers instead.
* Fascinators are basically something between a tiara and a head-dress. They are often adorned with one or two feathers and are a super-chic and stylish choice.
* Pins and clips covered with diamante, crystals or pearls look great when they catch the light and are wonderfully subtle.

DRESSING UP AND LOOKING GOOD

* Hats need not be the domain of the mother of the bride or groom! They are great with trendy trouser suits or dresses with a higher collar or jacket.

Veils

Most brides either love them or hate them but it's always a good idea to try one on – you might be surprised (or you'll have your mind more firmly made up that they are not for you)! Whether or not you wear it over your face and when and who lifts it are all down to you – tradition says the groom lifts it at the altar revealing his gorgeous bride but if you don't trust him with your hairdo, you could enlist the help of your Dad, Mum or bridesmaid. There are lots of lengths to choose from so it's best to try them on with your dress to see what goes best. Nylon veils will be stiffer than fine silk, which will 'drape' more and is also more pricey than manmade fabrics. Veils can be coloured, covered in jewels or decorated with embroidery – the choice is yours.

TAMRYN'S TIP

Veils are usually categorised in the following lengths (from shortest to longest): Shoulder, Waist, Hip, Floor, Train, Cathedral.

Jewellery

Most brides like to wear a necklace and/or earrings with their outfit. You could wear something that's been in your family for a long time or something that has a special meaning to you. Or, you could buy something just for the day. It's a good idea to take the shape of the neckline of your dress into consideration when deciding on jewellery. Chokers look fabulous with strapless dresses as they shorten the neck (which can be offset with drop earrings). If you're wearing a halter-neck gown, finding a necklace will be tough so you can just wear gorgeous earrings, maybe with a matching bracelet or a floral wrist corsage. Low necklines call for pendants while high necklines need delicate jewellery that doesn't interfere with the dress.

Bags

If you want to carry a bag (or just need an excuse for another one!), there are some wonderful wedding bags available. Sparkly bags or coloured bags will enliven a simple dress but a plain satin bag will go well with anything. You can get them in numerous shapes from buckets to clutches and decorated with everything from flowers to sequins and motifs. Once you've got your bag, pack it with wedding day essentials – face powder, lipstick, tissues and headache pills! However, a bag isn't essential. Most brides that do have them don't actually carry them throughout the day – they're usually just left somewhere so don't feel this is a 'must have' item.

Underwear

You needn't wear 'the full monty' of stockings and suspenders if you don't want to. In fact, if you have a slim-fitting dress, you may not be able to unless you want your guests to see the outline of everything! If you're wearing a strapless gown, you could go for a bra that is sewn into the gown or not bother with anything if your bodice is boned and well fitting. Basques look fab but might get hot in the summer and 'hold you in'. Knickers might give you the figure you need but won't do much for your sex appeal. If you need 'practical' undies during the day but still want to sizzle on the wedding night, you can always slip off and change just before the end of the proceedings. The main thing with wedding underwear is comfort – it's a long time to be stuck in something you're uncomfortable in and you can hardly adjust yourself over dinner! Hold-ups are a great alternative to stockings and tights but make sure you don't slap on too much body lotion before you put them on as this decreases their ability to hold up!

Buying from the High Street

Don't simply head straight to your local specialist bridal wear retailer, particularly if you're on a budget. High-street stores such as Debenhams and Monsoon have bridal wear collections that are surprisingly stylish and reassuringly purse friendly. They are more likely to have a range of sizes in stock and order times are often shorter than for 'traditional' designers. Plus, if you need alterations, they can often recommend people in the local area who can help you. The Debenhams gowns are designed by some great names including Jasper Conran and there are often co-ordinating shoes, tiaras and bridesmaids' dresses available too.

Buying from Overseas

Recently there has been much talk about buying your wedding gown from overseas because of the potential savings involved. However, before you rush onto a website promising cheaper gowns, there are a few things to consider:

* How much will shipping and import charges add to the overall cost of the dress?
* Where will you be able to take the dress for alterations?
* Is the gown authentic? Does it come with certificates of authenticity or tags? You need to be sure it isn't just a poor designer copy.
* Is the seller authorised by the designer to sell those gowns?

✳ Do you have any comeback if the dress isn't delivered in time or isn't right?

There's no right and wrong answer to these questions and every bride will feel differently about the potential inconvenience versus the potential savings involved. Just be sure you've investigated things fully before taking the plunge.

Buying 'Pre-loved' Gowns

If you're on a budget or if you simply don't want to spend hundreds on a dress you are only going to wear once, there's absolutely nothing wrong with looking at a once-worn or 'pre-loved' gown. On-line auctions or specialist resellers are a brilliant place to look and you might find the dress that you've fallen in love with at a much reduced price. Just be sure that the dress is in good condition, clarify postage costs and ask if it's been cleaned since its previous wearing (if not, you'll need to factor in that cost to your calculations).

Dressing the Groom

Although weddings are undoubtedly the bride's day, the men in the party shouldn't use this as an excuse to slack off! Looking good is just as important for the groom bearing in mind that he is in most of the photographs too. And, after all the effort that the bride has put in, the groom should pay her back by looking delicious as she says her vows.

Groom Options

There is more choice for guys now than ever before and whether the men opt for a formal morning suit or a trendy open-necked shirt and trousers, the choice is theirs. Most men hire their outfits from a high-street supplier, especially if they are wearing more formal outfits. If they are just wearing suits, it could be a great excuse to splash out on something new. While it's important to complement the 'look' of the wedding, the groom should not feel obliged to co-ordinate totally with any colour scheme – wearing a pink tie or waistcoat is not necessary! If the groom doesn't want to match, he should try blending and wearing a neutral colour such as cream. The same goes for flowers – the men's buttonholes can be exactly the same as the flowers in the bridal bouquet or the type of flowers can be kept but the colour changed or vice versa. Remember that the groom is not just there as an 'accessory' – it's his wedding day too so the bride shouldn't dictate what her chap will wear! It's also quite nice if the groom can stand out from the other men in the wedding party with a fancier buttonhole or a slightly different-coloured cravat or tie.

TAMRYN'S TIP

You should check any charges that would apply in case of damage or loss of items. If you're hiring everything including tie pins and cufflinks, it's quite possible that a little thing will go missing at some point during the proceedings so you need to know what you would be charged. Likewise, if you are hiring top hats, don't let the photographer talk you into the shot with everyone throwing their hats into the air!

A few more things to consider include:

* The guys should make an appointment with your chosen supplier so that the whole male wedding party can be measured for their outfits. If there are any children in the group, however, they can't be measured up until closer to the event in case they grow. Outfits are usually delivered to the store the week before the

wedding, so they can be tried on and there is time to get replacements if something doesn't fit well. Returns usually have to be made on the first weekday following the wedding, so if you are going on honeymoon, you'll need to make arrangements for someone else to return everything to avoid charges.

❊ Dress shoes (patent tipped) can also be hired but most grooms prefer to wear their own shoes to avoid blisters! Spend some time before the day cleaning them well as it's surprising how many photographs have feet in them. Generally, it's best to wear black shoes and everyone in the wedding party should try to stick to this – a pair of feet in another colour will really stand out in the pictures.

❊ Some couples like to provide matching cufflinks for everyone in the party, possibly showing the person's job title or the date of the wedding. This is a nice little touch and memento for the people concerned but isn't essential.

❊ Grooms should also have a little pre-wedding pampering – a good haircut is essential and some even get into tooth whitening and manicures for the big day – who said men don't care how they look??!

Looking Good for Girls

All brides want to look stunning on their wedding day, for their groom, for themselves and for the photographs that will stay with them forever. Good make-up will make all the difference and even if you don't really wear much in every day life, you should at least have a go with some new products before the day to enhance the radiant bride look (do try them out before the day though in case of allergic reactions). Here are my make-up hints and other tips on looking fantastic in your photographs.

Practise Before the Day

Whether you are doing your make-up yourself or being pampered by a professional, do have a run through before the day. You want to know exactly how much to apply and where to apply it to create the best look.

New Products?

If you fancy splashing out on some new products for the big day, it might be worth booking yourself an appointment at a make-up counter. You can explain to the consultant what you want and ask them to suggest some shades and colours. You might even get some freebies! Be sure to test them too – your wedding day is not the time to find out that you're allergic to something.

Powder

There is a fine line between looking matte and looking chalky. It's better to re-apply your powder throughout the day to combat any shine rather than go over the top before the ceremony.

Lips

If you are wearing a veil, go easy on the gloss otherwise you could end up with your veil stuck to your mouth! Layer your lipstick to help it last and keep it and the lip-liner soft otherwise it'll look too hard in photographs. Pale pink lipsticks will make teeth look whiter and darker lip colours will look even darker in photographs. Apply a little foundation or powder to your lips beforehand to help your lipstick stay in place.

Eyeshadows

Cream eyeshadows crease quite quickly so it might be better to use powders. You can also buy eyeshadow bases that help powders stay put perfectly.

Mascaras

Waterproof is essential in case of wedding day tears! Browns are softer than blacks and choose mascaras that only need one coat to avoid clumpy-looking eyelashes in close-up photos. If you warm your eyelash curlers with a hairdryer, it'll help keep the curl for longer.

Eyeliners

Gently blend eyeliner to avoid a harsh look and to make eyes look soft and romantic! White eyeliner inside your lower eyelashes will open your eyes and make you look more alert.

Blusher

Complete the 'blushing bride' look with a sweep of blusher or dab of cheek stain. Both should be applied to the fullest part of your cheeks (easy to find when you smile) and adding a little blusher to your cleavage and hairline is a good idea too. Blotting a little powder on top of your blusher will help it last.

Cover-up

A good concealer is a god-send to brides who don't sleep much the night before the big day! It should blend well with your skin tone to avoid any obvious marks.

TAMRYN'S TIP

If you are using concealer under your eyes, make sure it's not light reflecting or you will have white-ringed eyes in your photographs.

Eyebrows

Make sure they are well-groomed and tidy. Brush a spot of clear mascara through them or use a little Vaseline or hairspray!

Perfume

This might not be classed as make-up but this is a good place to add a few lines about it! Brides all have their own reasons for choosing their wedding day perfume and it's great to keep it personal. To let the fragrance linger, try layering the matching body wash and lotions as well as the perfume itself. Apply your perfume 15 minutes before you go outside so it doesn't evaporate in the outside air and if you can get hold of a tiny sample size, you can keep it in your bag (or your bridesmaid's!) to refresh yourself during the day.

Body Beautiful

Your wedding day is your 'day in the life' of a superstar – people are taking photos of you all the time, everyone is there to see you and you are the centre of attention. You also want your groom to fall over himself when he sees you gliding toward him because you look so scrummy. Also for a lot of brides, there is the honeymoon to think about and most want to look great for that too. If you want to use your wedding as an excuse to get yourself into tip-top form, here is my bride's guide.

Weight

Quite a few brides are keen to lose a little weight before their wedding day and this is completely understandable. It might be the catalyst you have needed for a while or you might have just made the decision. In either case, it's best to lose weight slowly and steadily rather than rely on crash diets or miracle products. Even something small like cutting out biscuits and crisps will make a difference over time and it's best to combine a diet with an exercise routine. A few brisk walks or not taking the lift or even joining a gym will give you a toned, firmer figure. If you add more fresh fruits and vegetables to your diet, it'll have the added benefit of improving your hair, skin and nails as well as your general health.

Skin

The cheapest way to improve your skin is to drink more water, at least two litres per day. Beauty experts recommend that you cleanse, exfoliate, tone and moisturise every day and use a face mask once or twice a week. Stress can play havoc with your skin and, as stress levels can be high in the run-up to a wedding, spending a bit of time looking after your skin is a good idea. Some brides also book themselves a facial or two before the big day. One thing to note, however, is that sometimes facials can cause a few spots (as the system cleanses itself) so having them too close to your wedding date might not be a good idea.

Hair

Lots of brides still grow their hair for their weddings and if you want to do this, you should start sooner rather than later! Keep your hair in good condition with regular trims. Hairdressers say that to get your hair in perfect wedding condition, you should start to condition it regularly at least six months before the big day. You could consider taking a vitamin supplement aimed at improving hair quality, but if you are improving your diet, you shouldn't need to do this.

TAMRYN'S TIP

For super shiny hair, continue rinsing for at least 30 seconds after your hair starts to squeak when you are washing out shampoo or conditioner. Dull hair is often caused by a build-up of product residue!

Hands and Nails

Everyone is going to look at your hands on your wedding day – to look at your rings or just to give your hand a little squeeze – so it's good to get your hands and nails in tip-top condition for this battering! Daily application of hand cream will make a big difference, especially over winter, when hands are dry. Massaging the cream into the nails can stimulate growth and will also condition your cuticles. Take some time over shaping your nails (only file in one direction) or have a manicure or two. French manicures are still the top choice for brides as they are sophisticated and elegant and won't detract from your wonderful rings.

Feet

You might think that you don't have to bother about your feet – wrong! Most wedding shoes will show a little foot and if you are going on a beach honeymoon, your toes are going to get quite a lot of exposure. Slathering on plenty of foot cream will soften your skin and cutting your nails across rather than shaping them will help avoid any uncomfortable toe nails. A pedicure before the day is a nice idea and lots of brides have their toe nails painted to be their 'something blue'.

Brows

Having your eyebrows professionally shaped will ensure that they frame your face perfectly. You can then carry on the good work at home with tweezers (use them after a hot bath when pores are open) or book yourself in for regular brow waxes.

Teeth

You will be smiling continually on your wedding day and with this in mind, you might want to consider some form of tooth whitening. Laser treatments are long lasting but very expensive while DIY kits are much cheaper although the effects do wear off when you stop using the products.

De-fuzzing!

Having your legs, underarms and bikini line waxed before the wedding will get you smoothly through the day and honeymoon. If you've not had a wax before, don't make your first appointment immediately before your wedding in case you have a reaction. Book yourself in for one a couple of months ahead of the big day as a trial before deciding if you want to do this before the wedding. If waxing doesn't appeal, a razor for your legs and underarms and a tweezer or hair removal cream for your bikini line will do the same job!

Pale and Interesting?

If you'd like to have a little colour for your wedding day, you have two options if a last-minute sunshine holiday is out of the question – fake tans or sunbeds. Fake tan is safer but some people don't take well to it and end up streaky or orange (you can still have a fake-tan disaster even if you go to a professional)! Sunbeds, however, give a better colour but there are potential health risks associated with prolonged exposure. If you use a sunbed, build your tanning time up slowly, aim for two sessions a week and exfoliate and moisturise well after each visit as this will help to stop your skin drying out.

Keep Calm!

Exercising in the run-up to the wedding is also a great idea for a number of reasons. Obviously, it helps you lose weight, keeps you healthy, tones your muscles, helps you sleep and keeps you calm. The endorphins that are released into your blood stream during exercise are natural 'happy pills' so a quick jog or power walk is perfect if you are starting to fret. Also, taking time out from the planning is a fabulous idea. Sometimes, your mind can work out a solution to a problem during exercise because you are more relaxed.

I know it can seem like there is an awful lot of pressure put on brides to look like models on their wedding day but really the object of the exercise is twofold – to make you feel great and to make you look like the best version of yourself possible. No groom wants to see a stranger heading down the aisle towards him so be true to yourself. Personally, I couldn't have worn an awful lot of make-up on my wedding day because I don't generally apply much and I wouldn't have felt comfortable. However, I knew that I needed some, so after a few trials, I found a style that suited. It's a learning process but it's also a great opportunity to try things that you wouldn't usually bother with. The perfect outcome from all of this, however, is for you to feel fabulous and for your new husband to agree – whatever you do to achieve that is up to you!

CHAPTER CHECKLIST

After reading this chapter, you should be feeling more informed about shopping for your dress and more knowledgeable about looking great on your wedding day. Here's a quick précis of the most important points:

※ Set aside plenty of time for dress shopping. Don't be made to feel bad by a store assistant and don't feel pressurised into placing an order.

※ Dresses that don't look great on the hanger can look completely different when you try them on.

※ There are plenty of options for veils, tiaras and other head-dresses. Try lots of styles before making a decision.

※ You don't have to buy your dress from a specialist store – there are high-street collections, on-line sellers or 'pre-loved' gowns available too.

※ The groom and male members of the wedding party aren't simply accessories to the bride – they should have plenty of input into choosing their outfits.

※ You will need to wear a little more make-up than usual on your wedding day so have a few trials beforehand.

※ Don't use untested products on your wedding day – test for allergic reactions well in advance.

※ Facials can be great, but as they draw out impurities, don't have one too close to your date.

※ Exercise and water – the two best bridal beauty tips ever!

Fourteen
It's All About the Detail!

It may be a cliché but it's true, guests really do notice the little details and it's these that can transform your wedding into a 'wow' wedding. Details don't need to be expensive but they need to be well thought out and as meaningful as possible to the couples involved. This chapter deals with the detail; what works, what's good, what's not and what people really love. There is plenty of information on dealing with constraints imposed by your budget or by your venue, so that come the big day, no-one will even notice.

Designing the Detail

Nowadays, there is much talk about 'Themes' and 'Colours' in wedding planning and talking about your theme is a favourite bridal conversation. But it can seem like a daunting task to choose one, or even to decide if you want one in the first place! The benefit of deciding on colours you would like to use on the day or even a theme for the event is that it does whittle down the options available to you, and when there are so many wedding-related products on the market, this can be a blessing. It also gives you a great base from which you can work. You just need to think about what you want before you start buying items or ordering flowers and decorations.

Colours

Deciding on a colour scheme or just picking one particular colour that you'd like to use on your day can help to bring everything together and create a sense of harmony and organisation. If you choose pink and ivory, for example, you could use pink flowers and ivory candles. The most popular colours to use in weddings seem to be gold, ivory, pinks, silvers and lilacs. However, if you want a bright orange scheme, go for it.

As long as you work with the 'Design Rules' opposite, you'll be fine. You might want colours that 'go' with your venue (i.e., pale pastels for a summery country house wedding or rich deep reds for a castle wedding in winter) or you might choose colours that mean something to you such as the colour of a dress you wore on a first date. You could just pick colours that you like and you know suit you! However, if you do decide on colours, do carry them through or otherwise it can look a little odd if most things are in co-ordinating colour with the exception of a few items.

Popular colours do change a little and a great place to look for inspiration is fashion magazines. See what colours will be popular next season and what styles everyone will be wearing. Is shabby chic or immaculate metro the way forward? Of course, you do need to consider your venue because there's no point trying to turn a sleek hotel into a retro haven. Look at the ideas that you have and select one that will complement you and your venue.

Themes

Some people love 'themed' weddings and others don't, but it's your day so if you fancy a 'Jane Austen' day with your man in breeches and you in a 'Pride and Prejudice' style gown, that's up to you. You don't have to go mad with themes, however – you can scale down a theme so it just works with, for example,

IT'S ALL ABOUT THE DETAIL!

table names, the cake and the pictures on your menus! To help guests to understand your theme, it's often a good idea to pick something with meaning or make a little joke about it during the reception – your Grandma is not going to understand why the cake is bright red unless she knows your new husband supports Liverpool FC!

Of course, you might like the idea of a theme but not know where to start, so use the questions below as prompts and see what ideas emerge:

* How did you both meet? Is there a city or location that could form the basis for your theme?
* What are your hobbies? Do you both love to travel or spend huge amounts of time at rugby matches?
* Do you have a specific love (apart from each other!)? Motor racing? A particular band? I've even worked on a wine-theme wedding for clients which was great fun.
* Is there any family history that you would like to incorporate? Are there any cultures that you would like to acknowledge?

The Design Rules

You have probably now got a clear idea of either colours or a theme, however loose, for your wedding so now it's time to consider the 'Design Rules' and think about how they will affect your decorations and details:

* Be a guest for a moment. Walk through your venue(s) the way that guests will. Are there any features you see that you want to highlight or disguise? The best way to disguise anything is to place something opposite it to draw the eye from things that aren't so picturesque. Alternatively, highlight a great view from a window with some decorations on the windowsills or light up a gorgeous fireplace with lots of candles and petals.

✳ Where will guests be the longest? If you are providing a meal for your guests, spend most of your time and budget in decorating the room that everyone will be eating in.

✳ Try to keep the space as 'open' as possible. Taller, more solid decorations are best placed around the edges of a room so that the central areas feel spacious. Remember that although rooms might look empty when you are planning they can quickly look crowded when you add guests, waiters, waitresses and other suppliers.

✳ Vary the eye line – a mix of low and tall table centres will provide more visual interest, particularly if you are having a more relaxed look. Ranks of identical arrangements suit a more modern style.

✳ Keep things in proportion. If your rooms have high ceilings, small, low table centres will be lost whilst taller arrangements will make the rooms look more enclosed.

✳ First impressions count so think what guests will see first when they enter. Something that makes them go 'wow' straight away is a great idea. This could even be a flower arrangement that is then moved to another location once everyone has arrived.

✳ Limit what guests have to notice. That probably sounds mad but it's better to place one great detail at each point (on entry to the venue, by the entrance to the dinner room, on the table etc.) than cram loads of items onto your table. You might have spent hours tying ribbons and tags onto lovely favour boxes but that detail will be lost if you then throw in table confetti, candles, petals, cameras and all the other essentials such as glasses, cutlery, crockery, salt, pepper, butter, water, wines …

✳ Look at unusual ways to present the usual. Table cameras for example have been really popular in recent years but they can stand out glaringly on tables that

IT'S ALL ABOUT THE DETAIL!

would look absolutely stunning without them. Think instead about placing a bowl full of cameras on the bar with a note asking people to use them. Be creative.

Flowers and Decorations

Flowers are still the most popular way of decorating a wedding venue, whether you opt for fresh or faux. There's something about gorgeous blooms and the way they can totally transform a space that is breathtaking, possibly because they always bring a touch of luxury to everything. Bear in mind that flowers can be expensive so use the 'Design Rules' to concentrate the effect where it will be most noticeable.

If you are working with a florist to bring the best to your venue, you should expect lots of advice and help so don't worry if you don't know your peonies from your pansies. The professionals are there to guide and help you create the best effect for your budget but here are some things to bear in mind when you are thinking floral:

* Remember that people need to see each other across the tables so towering arrangements in the centres are a bad idea.
* A swag of blooms hanging behind the top table will frame the happy couple wonderfully in photographs.
* Using seasonal flowers is a great way to cut costs. Speak to your florist for advice and remember that most flowers will increase in cost around Christmas, Valentine's Day, Easter and Mother's Day.
* Scented flowers might be great for your bouquet but think before using them on tables – will the aroma overpower the food?
* If you are having a colour theme, take fabric swatches or ribbons to your florist as it will help when choosing the perfect variety for your day.

* Make yourself feel good – how about donating your floral decorations to a local hospital or home after the celebrations?
* Don't like the idea of throwing your bouquet away? Get a smaller version made to fling to the waiting women!
* Red is popular for bouquets but there are plenty of alternatives to roses – gerberas, tulips, or even poinsettias for a winter wedding.
* Something blue? Include a few blue flowers in your bouquet or how about a choker or corsage with a blue delphinium, iris or hyacinth?
* Take pictures of any flowers you like to your florist as a starting point. Also, thinking about what you don't want can be just as useful.
* Write individual notes to your bridesmaids and have them attached to their bouquets as a thoughtful extra.
* Don't forget the foliage! Greenery is always important. Ivy is elegant and timeless or try beargrass or eucalyptus for a more contemporary look.
* Let the men express themselves! Get your buttonholes made in a variety of similarly coloured flowers; they can all pick their favourites.
* Alternatives to bridesmaid's bouquets are pomanders of tightly packed blooms. These are particularly good for children as they can hang from their wrist on a ribbon.
* Some varieties of lilies have pollen that stain and cause some people to sneeze. Most florists will remove pollen buds on flowers that have already opened when they deliver them but someone might need to tweeze out pollen from blooms that open during the day.
* Register offices often have fresh arrangements each day but if you really want to supply your own blooms, check with them first.
* Tea lights surrounded by scattered petals or bowls of floating candles and flowerheads are cost-efficient and elegant.

IT'S ALL ABOUT THE DETAIL!

* Seasonal fruits and vegetables can look fabulous. Try pumpkins as vases in autumn or add strawberries to arrangements in summer.
* Ask your florist what props they have in stock. If they need to buy lots of vases, stands or fabric, that will really increase costs.

Always be up-front with your florist about your budget. Most can tailor designs to suit your purse if they know how much you have to spend. They can also suggest 'dual use' arrangements so they can be moved from ceremony to reception which will help to keep the quote under control.

Styles

Before you visit your florist, make a list of the flowers, floral displays and possible quantities you think you will need. Also, write down details of flowers and styles you like to help you decide. If you have really got no idea what you like, take a photo of your dress, your venue and anything else because all of those things can help your florist make suitable suggestions. Refer to the list below for floral shopping list ideas:

* **Bridal bouquet:** hand-tied / wired shower / posy / a few dramatic flowers (calla lilies or grand prix roses) / wrist corsage. Do you want any replicas for tossing the bouquet or gifts?
* **Bridesmaid bouquet:** hand-tied / wired shower / posy / a few dramatic flowers (calla lilies or grand prix roses)/ wrist corsage / pomander / smaller version of bride's / contrasting.
* **Buttonholes:** who do you want to provide a buttonhole for? The wedding party only (bride, groom, best man, ushers, parents, page boy, readers etc.), or every wedding guest?

* **Church arrangements:** pedestal arrangements or other focal points / Arrangement for certain places / garlands over entrance to church or gate / swags for chair backs / pot-based arrangements for outside of the church / pew-end decorations.
* **Reception arrangements:** table centres / top table arrangement / arrangement to flank top table / cake table / general room decorations.

Alternatives

It can be tempting to go 'DIY' with flowers, especially if you are a bit of a floral buff but there are a few things to bear in mind before you decide to do everything. Where will you get all your flowers from? Most flower markets don't encourage 'public' buyers and concentrate on trade purchases. If you do find one that will supply you, you will have to be there at the crack of dawn and will probably have to pay in cash for your purchases. How will you transport the flowers? What other equipment will you need – wires, tapes, vases, foam, secateurs? When will you actually put the arrangements together? Most florists work flat out in the few days before the wedding putting everything together and even finish buttonholes and other highly perishable items hours before the wedding. Although you can make savings this way, be sure that you have got enough time for all the work and enough support to deal with the potential stress!

Of course, there are plenty of alternatives to flowers and most of these options work well if you want to put everything together yourself as they can be prepared and assembled well in advance of the day.

* **Candles:** these are always really popular. Place a group before a mirror for gorgeous flickering reflections or hire (or even buy cheap) candelabras and 'go grand'. Don't forget to light the edges of rooms with

candlelight to continue the soft romantic look. Tie colour co-ordinated ribbon around larger ones or use perfumed nightlights for a subtle scent.

* **Fairy lights:** gently twinkling, fairy lights are always atmospheric so wrap them around pillars, frame windows with them or use battery-powered light packs to add additional glow to simple table centres.

* **Balloons:** some people love them and some people don't but they are relatively inexpensive, they come in any colour you care to mention and they certainly say 'party'.

* **Jewels:** for a really decadent feel, thread glittering jewels onto invisible wire and snake them across tables, swag them across the front of the top table or suspend them from suitable spots.

TAMRYN'S TIP

Before you go out and buy candleholders or similar, firstly check that your venue allows their use and then ask if they have anything you can use! Quite a few have stocks of tea light holders or even larger candelabras they might let you use for the occasion.

Tables

If you talk to any excited bride, most will be able to talk for an almost indecent amount of time about how they are going to decorate their tables! There are some absolutely brilliant ideas out there at the moment and if you have got the courage to be creative you have literally got unlimited scope to do whatever you like. Just remember to keep it simple. Be wary about going over the top, which can be tough when you see so many great ideas but think carefully about the look you want to achieve. Resist buying things for your tables just because it seems to be 'the done thing'. Ultimately, you don't need any of these things, they're just nice (okay, lovely!) extras, but you've got a budget to stick to and you want to create the maximum impact, so steer clear of clutter.

Table Centres

Of course, if you are having floral table centres, your florist will be a great source of ideas and you can do anything from a single perfect flower in a tall vase to low arrangements circling candles, blooms floating in bowls of water or flowers falling from iron candelabras. Any colour, any style and any budget – it's possible to have flowers to suit any occasion. However, it's becoming more popular for table centres to comprise of other items so here are a few ideas for you. Just keep in mind the 'Design Rules' and always think about the size of the tables and the size of the rooms and you can do many more things than you would expect.

* **Candles:** bowls featuring floating candles or groups of candles at various heights, surrounded by petals in the centres of tables can look stunning. Tiny tea lights are very effective but can get lost on their own so you might need to think of other things to complement them.
* **Twisty twigs:** branches of twisted willow, spray-painted, look excellent as centrepieces. Place them in a vase or container and add fairy lights, glitter, flower heads or even baubles for a winter wedding.
* **Edible treats:** for a more relaxed-style reception or for children's tables, how about edible centrepieces? Buckets or bowls filled with lollipops or chocolates look and taste great.
* **Wire and light:** this is a great look for contemporary weddings. Lay spirals of coloured wire along the centre

　　　　IT'S ALL ABOUT THE DETAIL!

of the table, thread fairy lights along the base and cover with petals.

TAMRYN'S TIP

Highlight your table centre by using some fabric underneath. Choose a colour to complement your theme and loosely fold it and stand your centrepiece on top. This is a really inexpensive way of making cheaper table centres look much more luxurious.

Favours

Favours started out as an Italian tradition – five sugared almonds (a symbolic mix of sweetness and bitterness) given to represent health, happiness, fertility, wealth and longevity. This has now evolved into many variations of little gifts, left on tables for guests during the dinner. However, while they are nice to give and receive, if your budget doesn't stretch to them, don't worry – you could just have a bowl of chocolates on the tables or not bother with them at all. Most favours can be personalised with the guest's name in some way so that they can also double up as place cards. Some people give different favours to men and women, but again, this is up to you. I have listed some ideas below:

* **Favour boxes:** these can be filled with any variety of sweets (chocolates, love hearts, almonds, dragees (coated almonds or chocolate), jelly beans – the list is endless) and decorated with ribbons, feathers and flowers.
* **Candles:** part-favour and part-table decoration! Candles are always popular and little tea light holders

can be personalised with the guests' names and your details. The variety of candles available is endless.

* **Alcohol miniatures:** always popular! Little bottles of whisky, port, wine, or even 25cl bottles of bubbly if you are feeling generous.

* **Lottery tickets:** it could be one of your guests! Lucky dip tickets or scratchcards in personalized envelopes would double as place cards.

* **Toiletries:** bath bombs, little soaps, even mini bottles of perfumes look great nicely wrapped and ribboned. Bath confetti would be very apt!

* **Seeds:** little packets of seeds in decorated mini terracotta pots which will grow as your marriage does.

* **Biscuits:** shaped biscuits wrapped in cellophane or just decorated with ribbons make yummy favours. They could also have guests names iced onto them to double up as place markings.

* **More sweeties:** individual chocolates with a little flag stuck in as a place card, brightly coloured jelly beans in an etched shot glass or personalised sticks of seaside rock.

* **CDs:** you could make up a CD for each guest of 'Wedding Hits' including your favourite songs, music you played during your ceremony and even your first dance tune.

* **Favours for children:** as it's not appropriate for younger children to have favours, you could make them up a little goody bag to keep them entertained – pencils, papers, activity books, bubbles, even a cuddly toy! Making up a 'wedding quiz' perhaps with word searches or questions about the day would keep older kids amused. You could even offer a prize for the winners. Similarly, a colouring competition for younger children would be great – find a suitable piece of wedding clip art on your PC, enlarge it and print it out.

When it comes to favours, anything goes as everyone always loves a gift! The only limit is your budget and your imagination. Just remember that they are not essential so if you would rather spend your money elsewhere, go ahead. As much as guests will notice a nice favour at their place, they won't notice if there isn't one.

TAMRYN'S TIP

Be sure to let your guests know they can take their favours home otherwise you will be left with lots at the end of the night.

Place Cards

If you've gone to the trouble of working out a seating plan, you will need place markers to guide guests to the correct spot at their table. The 'norm' for place markers are simple small tented cards upon which is written the guest's name, but of course, there are plenty more options open to you than that!

* ✳ **Favour combination:** add a tag to each guest's favour and set it at their place. They will definitely know the favour is for them!
* ✳ **Nice and natural:** rustic or country themes need the entire look to be as 'outdoorsy' as possible. Think about using leaves with names handwritten on, or pebbles painted with guests' names. Little cards poking out from fir cones or even pinned onto fruit are also great ideas.
* ✳ **Menu combo:** it's quite popular to combine place markers with menus as well. The guest's name is written at the top with the menu underneath and this card is then laid at the correct place.

* **Hanging markers:** chairs are the perfect place to put your markers and by having them there, less space is taken up on the table itself. Thread a card onto some ribbon and tie it onto each chair.

Napkins

Another piece of tableware that is commonly overlooked until the venue twists or rolls them into shapes that completely ruin the look of your tables. If you have put a lot of thought into how the table should look and then everything is completely overpowered by swan-shaped napkins, it's a real shame. So, don't overlook them, include them!

* A simply folded napkin looks incredibly elegant. If you have got a menu card or favour inside an envelope, a pocket fold will allow the item to be slipped inside for the guest to find without dominating the look of the table.
* One of the most popular napkin styles is an easy roll. You can then tie the napkin with ribbon and even attach a place card if you like before laying the finished item at the place setting.
* A new way to display your napkin is to fold it once or twice then lay it over the edge of the table so that it drapes down over the edge of the table (this looks even

more effective when you use coloured napkins) – favours, place cards or menus can be placed on top.

TAMRYN'S TIP

If you are planning on doing something with your napkins, make sure you let your venue know! Ask the venue to leave the napkins unfolded for you so that you can do with them as you wish as soon as you or your helpers arrive to set up.

Table Top Details

As mentioned in the 'Design Rules', you do need to be careful about adding too many 'busy' details to your table tops as they can really detract from other items. So, before you splash out on more petals, metallic table confetti or anything else, think carefully as to whether they are actually going to make things look better. But if you can't resist, think about using them for the evening reception only when tables will be less crowded than at dinner.

Numbers or Names?

There has been a big trend recently to give each table a name rather than a number. The idea behind this is that it stops guests feeling affronted that they're sitting on table 14 when another friend or relative is on table two. However, it's always obvious, whatever you do, if a table is close or not to the top table, so don't think that simply giving a table a name, not a number, will solve this! That said, table names can be great fun and if you are having a theme through the day, they give you a great opportunity to continue this. Places you have visited together, films, stars, songs, football clubs, cars or any group you care to mention can be used and they are always great talking points for guests. Numbers work just as well, but if you are having a large wedding, most table plans always leave out the number 13.

TAMRYN'S TIP

Remember that the table name or number cards displayed on your tables have to be big enough and high enough for guests to be able to read when they enter. A5 is the usual size for these. Also consider writing the name or number on both sides of the card so the table is easily spotted, whichever way the card is facing.

Stationery

Wedding stationery can be a surprisingly large expense for many couples. Because of this, some decide to make their own. If you go down that route, remember to leave yourself lots of time because making 100 or so invitations and all the other accessories can take longer than you expect. Also, if you are planning on doing this as a cost-saving exercise, be sure that after you've bought all the equipment you need, you are still saving money! Professionally made items are still very popular and there are styles and prices to suit everyone from the traditional letterpress styles to handmade or more modern designs featuring gorgeous images. Be sure to take your time when choosing and make sure that whatever you choose will complement the style of wedding you are planning. For example, heavy card invitations in swirling script are perfect for more traditional events, whilst the clean graphic ranges are great for more contemporary weddings.

TAMRYN'S TIP

If possible, order all your stationery at once because many suppliers offer discounts for 'bulk buys'. This also ensures that all the stationery co-ordinates and you are not worried about designs being discontinued.

Invitations

You will need one invitation for each family group or couple that you are going to invite and also a few 'spares' in case of mistakes or additional guests. Remember that it's only the people named on the invitation who are officially invited so don't state 'The Lawson Family' if you don't want children to attend. Formally worded invitations invite 'Mr and Mrs' or you can call people by their Christian names if you are going for a more informal day. Remember that invitations are the guests' first clue to the style of the event so make sure your invitations give the right signals. See page 135 for more information on invitations.

TAMRYN'S TIP

For civil ceremonies, most registrars object to you using the phrase 'Order of Service' as this is a religious term and deemed inappropriate for civil weddings.

Orders of Ceremony

If you are providing an order of ceremony, whether it's for a religious or civil ceremony, you can easily get away with one between two and there is no need to provide them for every person present. Of course some will be taken as keepsakes but huge over-ordering here is something to avoid. Speak to whomever is taking your ceremony for information on what can be included and make sure that the content is approved before you print!

Table Plans

The usual format for a table plan is one big mounted card listing each table and the guests seated at it. You can decorate this any way that you wish but make sure that the writing is large enough to read from a distance and if you have got a larger number of guests, consider having two on display to save a crowd forming in front of one! Put them somewhere where they will be noticed to give people time to find their details before dinner.

TAMRYN'S TIP

The new trend is for small cards which show the guest's name and their table assignment individually. Guests can pick them up from a designated table and they can be displayed in many ways – attach them to favours to guarantee all are taken or just line them up alphabetically for guests to find.

Menus

Unless you are combining menus with place cards, there is really no need to provide one menu per guest – one or two per table will certainly suffice. Before you order them, speak with your venue as most will be able to provide menus for you – they may not be exactly as you'd wish but they'll do the job and save you some money if your priorities lie elsewhere.

Thank-you Notes

Of course you should say 'thank you' to guests after the event, whether or not they buy you a gift. People have still made the effort to attend and you should certainly thank them for their attendance. Again, one per couple and a few spares is plenty to order. Thank-you notes should go out within six weeks of the wedding. There is no need to write essays for each – a short simply worded note sent promptly is much nicer than a longer, later effort.

CHAPTER CHECKLIST

Hopefully this chapter will have left you feeling inspired and full of ideas. Just remember to focus on a few of these details and don't feel that you have to make every element absolutely stunning. Overkill and over-design ends up making things look too contrived and it's impossible for guests to notice every detail properly. Keep the following in mind:

✳ Your florist should be your floral encyclopaedia. Listen to their advice and be as clear with them as you can about what you want and how much you have to spend.

✳ Remember the 'Design Rules' on page 199 because they will help you put together a great-looking event on any budget.

✳ Avoid the temptation to over-dress your tables. Remember that things will get hugely more crowded when cutlery, crockery, glasses and everything else is added.

✳ Doubling up is a great way to keep tabletops clearer – combine favours with place markers, for example, for a more refined look.

✳ Avoid over-ordering on your stationery. You might not mind having cake or favours left over but piles of invitations or orders of ceremony can't really be used for anything else!

Fifteen
Suppliers

It's clear to see that your wedding will take a lot of planning, but at some point you have to hand these plans over to other people to execute for you. This is why the wedding suppliers that you choose to be involved in your day will have such a huge influence on the occasion – surround yourself with good suppliers and your life will be a lot easier. This chapter will give you information on how to book the suppliers that are best for you both, regardless of your budget, your location or the style of your wedding.

Wedding Day Workers

It's safe to say that the people who will be there on the day itself are the suppliers that have the most impact on the success of the event. Wedding day workers include the following:

* Photographer
* Videographer
* Florist
* Musicians
* Caterer (if applicable)
* Cake maker
* Hair and make-up artist
* Other entertainers
* Chauffeurs
* Wedding planner/Wedding co-ordinator

Of course, from that list, there are some people that you and your guests will be interacting with more so they are even more important. Photographers, videographers, entertainers and wedding co-ordinators will have more of a 'public' role on the day whereas florists, caterers and similar are likely to go unseen by the majority of guests. It goes without saying that you need to trust all of these people implicitly – worrying about their capabilities or whether they will turn up on the day is not something that you need to be doing!

As these suppliers can only work on one wedding per date, these are the people that you should be booking first after you have booked your ceremony and your venue. Lots of 'wedding day workers' take on clients two or three years in advance so researching and subsequently booking professionals from this category shouldn't really be put off too long.

Behind the Scenes

There are also numerous individuals who will be contributing to your wedding without being there on the day or even meeting you beforehand! These 'behind the scenes' suppliers could provide:

* Stationery
* Jewellery and tiaras
* Shoes, bags and accessories
* Favours and table decorations
* Hired items such as table linen, glassware, etc.
* Gifts or children's goody bags

The list here could be endless and the number of companies involved will depend on your plans for the day.

Although you won't be interacting with these people to the same degree as your 'wedding day workers', you'll still be handing over your hard-earned cash so you need to ensure that they are reliable, trustworthy and that their product is of good quality. It's all too easy, especially when you are pushed for time or eager to make some wedding-related purchases, to order too quickly without making sure that what you are buying is right for you. Remember that although these purchases are likely to be relatively low value, buying something that you don't use or isn't right is a complete waste of your money.

Unlike 'wedding day workers', your supporting suppliers aren't restricted by their availability on your wedding date. A favour company, for example, could easily supply favours to 100 brides all getting married on the same day without any problems so there is not such a need to book or order from these companies so early. Of course, they do still have some limits, particularly when things have to be made in advance (tiaras, stationery or similar) but it's highly unlikely that you will need to order these items years in advance to make sure they arrive in time for your wedding day!

Researching Suppliers

Researching your suppliers is absolutely critical and I can't stress enough that time spent on this task won't be wasted. You shouldn't plump for the first photographer you find, simply because they are within your budget. I know that sometimes feelings of desperation kick in and you feel under pressure to make a booking quickly but this can backfire on you further down the line when you realise you are not totally comfortable with your choice.

There are numerous ways to research suppliers. You can ask friends or relatives for recommendations, browse wedding magazines, go to trade associations and professional bodies or spend some time on the internet hunting for websites. Call or e-mail the companies that you initially like the look of and ask for more information, although this isn't always necessary if you are looking at their websites. When you have received the information, take some time to read everything thoroughly and keep the following in mind:

* Was your enquiry answered promptly? If you are not treated well at this initial contact when they should be working to attract your business, how will you be dealt with once they have got you to sign on the dotted line?
* Is their material well put-together? Spelling mistakes and other errors don't bode well for someone's attention to detail.
* What impression do you have of this supplier? And is it an impression that you like? If you are a very laid back, informal person, would incredibly formal communications make you feel a little uneasy or vice versa?
* Is the service or product described something that meets your requirements? Do you need it and are you happy with what is included in the cost?
* Does the cost described fit your budget? If it's slightly over, how do you feel about cutting back elsewhere?
* For 'wedding day workers', are they available on your wedding day?

Meeting Suppliers

Once you have weeded out some companies from your initial list, you'll need to take things further with the ones that you are interested in. Obviously, for stationery or table decorations, the next step might well be to order the products, but for your 'wedding day workers', arrange to meet people to get a good feel for them, their work and their ideas for your wedding day. These meetings should take place at your convenience but it might be easier for you to visit photographers or florists at their studios so that you can view portfolios, albums and samples. At your meeting, there are literally hundreds of questions that you can ask but you'll usually find that the supplier will cover most of these naturally. Here are some things that you should remember about these meetings:

✽ When you meet with suppliers, take a list of questions that you want to ask so you don't leave and then realise you have forgotten crucial points. Write down their answers so you have a record.

✽ Make the most of your 'real time' with suppliers to view portfolios and confirm details. Trying to do this via telephone or e-mail can take ages and it's harder to be precise about what you want this way.

✽ Check that the person you have been dealing with is the person that will be there on the day itself. Knowing the supplier and being able to build rapport with them is brilliant from both sides of the relationship – you feel comfortable that they will do a great job and they will understand you and your wishes a lot better.

✽ Be very specific about what you want and communicate clearly – write down your ideas or use pictures from magazines to show styles you like. Don't be afraid to make suggestions and ask for advice or opinions.

✽ Read through every contract before you sign it and question anything you are not happy with before you do. Make sure costs and payment times are noted down, as well as any additional costs for travel, food or even accommodation, so there are no surprises later on.

✽ Don't ever feel bad if you want to ask for references from suppliers; they should be happy to have someone sing their praises for them. Make sure the references are recent and, if references are not forthcoming, ask yourself why.

✽ Never 'assume' suppliers will know what you want. If you want a photo with the girls from university or if you need a layer of your cake to be gluten-free, let people know. Suppliers really do want every client to be happy so ask for exactly what you want.

✽ For 'creative' suppliers such as florists or cake makers, be clear about your budget from the start. This will allow them to design a package that will fit your requirements and stay within your budget.

TAMRYN'S TIP

Feeling comfortable with your 'wedding day workers' is absolutely critical. There are plenty of suppliers who essentially offer the same services at the same price but you need the one that you are happiest with.

Depending on the supplier concerned, there are other things to keep in mind as well and I have listed these below.

Photographers

This is likely to be the only time that you commission a photographer so ask as many questions as you like – no question is a silly question. Make sure that the sample albums you see are from the photographer who will be snapping away on your day and that an album is actually from one entire wedding, not just a collection of the best images from a number of events.

Videographers

The sample video you are sent should be a complete wedding as you need to know how important moments such as the ceremony and speeches are handled. If you are looking for something more creative, look again at the company literature – is there a strong style and sense of flair?

Florists

Make sure that images in their portfolio are photos of their work, not simply cuttings from magazines. There should be a range of styles, not similar work reproduced in a variety of colours. Will you be expected to provide vases, ribbons, fabrics and little accessories or will the florist source these?

Cake Maker

Ask for samples because the taste of the finished product is as important as the look of the cake. If you are serving cake for dessert, you will need more than if you are simply using it for nibbles so be sure to tell your cake maker. If you want certain colours, provide swatches or samples. Always check if there are delivery costs involved.

Entertainment

Check that they're fully insured and that all of their electrical equipment is PAT tested (some venues insist on this). Just giving your musical entertainers an idea of your style should be enough for them to put together a dance floor filling playlist. Obviously mention any songs that you really do or don't want to be played but try to avoid giving them a song by song description of the night – you should be confident enough in their abilities to trust they'll 'get it right on the night' for you.

Wedding Co-ordinator

This is the person who will ultimately be responsible for the running of your wedding day so you need to trust them totally. Someone who is late for meetings, disorganised with paperwork or forgetful isn't someone who is going to make you feel that everything is under control. Experience really counts here, so ask for references, look at their portfolios and ask them for as many suggestions as you like – they should always be able to offer alternatives and help you out when you are having a 'will it work?' crisis.

Ultimately, your choice of supplier is a very personal thing and some of that decision will be made on gut instinct. Just make sure that you ask plenty of questions before you commit yourself so that you can feel totally at ease with all of your suppliers.

Put together a list of contact details for all your suppliers and give each of them a copy. So, if the cake maker needs to talk to the florist or the photographer to the chauffeur, they can without having to use you as a go-between.

Negotiating Skills

One of the questions that I'm most frequently asked is 'Can we negotiate with suppliers?'. I would say that there's no harm in trying but don't be offended if they say no and don't take that as a signal of their competence – it might mean that they're very busy and don't have to use discounts to get bookings or that they are already offering a competitive price and can't reduce it without wiping out all their profit (wedding suppliers need to make money to live as well!). It can be tough to see a photographer charging £1000 for their services, but remember they are not making that much money from your day. When you factor in equipment, printing costs, films, albums, software, insurance, travel and their time (not just on the day but time for pre-wedding meetings, then post-wedding sorting, developing, enhancing and putting together a quality album), the cost is suddenly more understandable.

You might be luckier in your negotiating if your wedding is a weekday because a supplier could take another booking for the weekend. Sunday and Friday weddings are now almost as popular as Saturday nuptials so don't expect that they would attract a discount. Likewise, weddings aren't as seasonal as they used to be – Christmas and winter weddings are very popular and suppliers tend to squeeze holidays into months such as January and November.

Sometimes, asking for money off the whole package isn't the way forward so you could try to get one aspect reduced instead.

A videographer might be more willing to give you a reduced price on extra copies than money off the package price.

Suppliers that are newer to the marketplace might be willing to offer a lower price if you will agree to be included in their portfolio or give references. Just remember that if the service isn't high quality, you are not obliged to sing their praises simply because they shaved a little bit off their fee.

CHAPTER CHECKLIST

Choosing suppliers is ultimately a very personal thing – even if a few couples were looking for a photographer who would provide 65 photos in an album for a certain price, it's likely that each would book someone different simply because they felt more at ease with that professional. Trust your instinct but don't forget to question!

✽ Book your 'wedding day workers' early because these suppliers can only attend one wedding per day so once they are booked, it's too late.

✽ Read through a company's literature carefully. Do you like their style? Is it creative? Is it well put together?

✽ Research your suppliers thoroughly and spend time checking them out. Once you have signed the contract, you don't want to have second thoughts.

✽ Suppliers aren't mind readers so make sure you tell them what you want. If you've got a great rapport with them, these conversations should be brilliant because you'll be able to share ideas and learn from their experience.

✽ Don't feel bad if a supplier doesn't respond as you had hoped to your 'any chance of a discount?' approach. It doesn't mean that they don't want the work and it doesn't mean that they are not right for you. Be wary about having to rely on discounts to stay on budget – it's a very dangerous (and stressful!) game to play.

Sixteen
Etiquette and Expectations

Weddings can be stress inducing for many reasons but the two main causes of pre-marital headaches are the associated etiquette and expectations and the fact that for most couples, this day is the first and last large-scale event that they will plan. Put those factors together and it's not surprising that everything can be rather worrying and confusing so this is a chapter focused on the planning basics – read this, refer back to it regularly and you will be a wedding expert in no time at all!

Etiquette and Tradition

As we have already seen in most of the previous chapters, there is a huge amount of wedding etiquette and tradition. This can make you feel like you are never going to get the day you want, rather it will be more of a carbon copy of a million other weddings. Although some of the dilemmas below have been mentioned in other chapters, these are the questions that make up most of my queries from clients and other couples I speak to, so take comfort that you are not alone and not everyone does things by the book!

The ceremony is the part of the day that most people want to be 'right' – they're happy to do some unexpected things at the reception but the ceremony is sacrosanct – or is it? You can change things to suit yourself and it won't take anything away from the event at all. In fact, it will probably add to it because you will be happier and it will be more of a reflection of you both. Doing something simply because 'it's the done thing' won't make your wedding day better, doing something because you both want to include it will. So, if you are wondering whether you are the only person who isn't keen on wearing a veil or being given away or if you are still unsure about straying from the norm don't be – trust me, I'm a wedding planner!

Don't Give Me Away!

There is absolutely no reason why you have to be given away if you don't want to be, or if deciding who will accompany you up the aisle will cause problems. Quite a few modern brides aren't keen on the historical notion of being passed from one man to another and prefer to go to their groom as an equal. Some still like to be walked up the aisle, if only to have someone to hang onto, while some are accompanied by both parents which is a lovely touch and a great way to involve your mum in the day.

Attendant Anguish

If you don't want bridesmaids, best men or ushers, you don't need them. But if you don't have official attendants, you will still need to split their responsibilities among various people otherwise your task of planning the wedding will be much tougher. Your bridesmaids don't have to walk behind you up the aisle if you don't want them to and there is certainly no rule that says you need bridesmaids either.

Veils

A veil does not have to be part of your wedding outfit if you don't want it to be. If you do decide to wear one, you don't have to go along with the tradition that says the groom will lift your veil for you. You can lift it yourself or not even have it covering your face in the first place – after all, your groom should know what you look like by the time you hit the ceremony!

It may be 'expected' of you to do certain things at your reception but there is no reason to do things you don't want. As with all things wedding related, there is no definitive list of things you have to do to have a 'perfect' wedding and remember that your perfect wedding is probably not going to be someone else's which really is the whole point!

Do You Invite Suppliers to the Meal?

Standard etiquette may be to invite the vicar to your reception but it's unlikely that the registrar will expect this (and remember that two registrars will attend). If any of your suppliers request that you provide food (or if you just want to be kind) you certainly do not have to seat them with the guests. Most will be over the moon with a few sandwiches and a little sit down in peace for a moment.

TAMRYN'S TIP

If you are providing food for suppliers, clarify with your venue how this will be billed. Will it be a flat fee per head added to your final bill or will the exact costs be added to your room tab? Also, will you provide drinks or will the suppliers have to buy their own? Be clear about what you want to do before the day so you are not bothered with questions.

Cash Bars

Cash bars at receptions are very common these days and you shouldn't feel at all bad about asking guests to pay for their own drinks. It can stop a lot of problems with people over indulging if they are paying! If your reception is somewhere out of the way, it's a good idea to let people know in advance so that they can bring cash. This is especially important if there aren't any nearby banks or cash dispensers.

Cake Cutting

Etiquette says the cake should be cut after the meal but if you would prefer to cut your cake in the evening so that extra guests can be a part of this, that is perfectly acceptable. Alternatively, you could cut a traditional cake during the meal and order something like a chocolate cake for people to nibble on during the evening.

Getting Away From It All

You have arranged and paid for a wonderful party, all your family and friends are with you and yet tradition says you have to leave halfway through! You certainly don't have to do this if you don't want to – you can stay and party all night, it's up to you. If you are not going to leave halfway through, however, do let guests know in advance as some guests, especially older ones, might be waiting for you to leave before they do as etiquette demands.

Some 'Bride and Groom' Time

Yes, yes, we know the temptation is there to sneak off at some point of your reception to have some 'quality time' but it's actually considered quite rude to do this. Your guests are there for you, they have put themselves out to attend and most will be quite hurt if you disappear. You have the rest of your lives together (not to mention your first night together) so think twice before running off.

The Money Minefield

As we saw in the early chapter on budgeting, talking about money is never a great topic of conversation but of course, there are also expectations surrounding this too. I've highlighted some issues opposite.

Traditional

If you are having a 'traditional' wedding with regards to money, the burden of responsibility lies with the bride's parents. They pay for any engagement announcements in newspapers, all the wedding stationery, the bride's and bridesmaids' outfits, flowers and other decorations, photography or videography fees, transport, and the reception including the cake, food and drinks. The groom and his family have an easier time of it and are expected to pay for the engagement and wedding rings, ceremony fees, venue fees associated with the marriage ceremony, buttonholes, gifts for the attendants, the first night hotel and the honeymoon.

Modern

Modern couples, however, don't often stick to these 'rules'. Lots of couples decide to finance their entire wedding themselves or pay for things with some help from their families. Some families just give the couple a set amount of money to use as they see fit or they decide at the outset to pay for certain items. Whatever you decide to do, it's best to work out who will pay for things and what they can afford before you go out and order a £500 designer cake and make your parents pass out!

Money = Power?

This is a tricky one but not everyone has this problem so please skip this section if your familial relations are harmonious! Unfortunately, some families attach conditions to the money they will put into a wedding. For example, 'We'll pay for the food but we want to add 12 people to your guest list'. If that's okay with you both then there are no problems, but if it's not, it can cause ructions. The best thing to do is gently explain your constraints with regard to numbers and how you'd like to be in control of your guest list. Offer some compromise (they could attend just the evening reception), or if there's no room for movement, you might have to swallow that financial responsibility yourselves to regain control.

Money as Gifts

This is still frowned on by some people but if you ask for cash and people send cheques before the wedding – don't cash them until afterwards! It will look like you are using that money to finance your wedding. If you do need to bank them to pay for a honeymoon or the like, it might be a good idea to call the sender and let them know that the cheque has been deposited as you need it for a certain reason.

Family Issues

As the saying goes 'you can't choose your families' but there is sure to be a moment in the wedding build-up when you wish you could. Often, they don't realise they are upsetting you but on the odd occasion, comments can be a little thoughtless, petty and sometimes downright cruel. Here is how to keep your head when all about you are losing theirs.

Future Sister-in-Law = Bridesmaid?

In the past, all the couple's unmarried sisters were bridesmaids (it was thought to be a good way to 'show them off' to potential suitors) but now bridesmaids are much more often friends. If you really don't want your groom's sister to be a bridesmaid, don't ask her otherwise you might start to resent it. You could maybe find her another job such as doing a reading or as an usher.

Step Families

This is one of the biggest modern wedding etiquette headaches – who sits where, who'll make the speech, who'll be upset if someone else does something. All of these situations need careful handling as everyone wants to be important on the day. If the question of a top table is becoming too tricky, you could scrap it and place one couple from the bridal party on each table to act as 'host'. The key here is compromise and communication. You need to explain to families that you'd really appreciate their support on this day and they should be willing to compromise on a few things for the sake of your happiness. No-one wants any form of bad feeling on the day so be sure to clear everything up beforehand and explain your ideas to everyone – your big day is not the time for surprises!

Mothers and Mothers-in-Law

Both can be tricky! Some mums throw themselves into the planning and try to take over. If this isn't what you want, you need to tackle it tactfully before it gets out-of-control. Find her one (time-consuming!) task and say how you would love her to deal with it for you or take the bull by the horns and explain it's your day. If the bride's parents are paying, it might be tough but cash shouldn't be given with conditions attached. She might just be trying to plan the dream wedding that she didn't have, so go gently. Mothers-in-law can also suffer from that problem, or worse, they can suffer from disinterest (as can mums too to be honest). If this seems to be happening, don't push them. If it's attention seeking, depriving them of the attention they want (i.e., you constantly calling them telling them of plans) should help this pass. If it's genuine disinterest, it's much harder – the best course is often just to stop trying to drag them into the plans if that's not what they want as you will only end up being dragged down too.

Who Wears the Buttonholes?

Tradition says everyone in the bridal party – groom, best man, ushers and parents – should wear a buttonhole and it is a nice way of letting them stand out from the other guests. Men should wear them on the left and women on the right, but it's a lot more flexible with women who can put them on whatever side is more practical or attractive. You could provide more elaborate corsages for the mothers or even provide a buttonhole for every guest – it's your choice.

Customs

From garters to coins in your shoes, there are hundreds of wedding related customs and if you followed them all, you would never find time on the day to actually get married. So don't worry if someone says 'Oh dear, aren't you doing … ?' It's not the end of the world or the end of your relationship! Having said that, some of them are rather sweet and the majority of couples do stick to a few of these ancient customs as well as bringing in a few new ones.

A Best (Wo)man?

If the groom's best friend is a woman, she can certainly take up the position of the best man in a 'best woman' role. The job is really there to support the groom, help him out during the planning, produce the rings at the right moment and make a great speech. There is absolutely no reason why this person couldn't be a woman. A woman on a stag night might prevent some of the more 'fleshy' options! Most people at the wedding would know that they are close friends so it's hardly going to be a shock. Conversely, the bride can certainly have a 'man of honour' to help her out too.

Quick! The Americans are Coming!

Lots of US TV shows have got many of you thinking whether you need a 'shower' before your wedding and what's this fuss with rehearsal dinners? To answer these questions – bridal showers still aren't popular in the UK as we stick with the traditional 'hen do'. If you do want to try one, go ahead but it could very easily just turn into a second hen night (which might not be a bad thing!).

Rehearsal dinners are beginning to catch on in the UK, especially when family groups stay in a hotel the night before the wedding. In the US, after the wedding rehearsal, everyone has dinner and a little party, sometimes gifts are given and speeches and toasts are made. The groom's parents usually pay for it and it is quite a good way for the main participants in the ceremony to get to know each other better. If most of the wedding party will be in the one place, a rehearsal dinner will be really easy to organise and is a friendly, happy way to spend the night before the big day.

Seeing your Intended on the Morning

This is supposed to bring bad luck, but if you live together, one of you might not want to decamp for the night. It might give you lots of reassurance that everything's okay or seeing them might just make you more nervous. Whatever you decide, it won't bring you any better luck than the other option. Likewise, a quick phone call or text message on the morning of the day won't be a harbinger of doom either.

Bouquets Away!

The custom of throwing your bouquet into a crowd of eager women to determine who'll marry next is still going strong. However, brides who've paid a fortune for their bouquet or have plans for it after the wedding will probably not be so keen. You can scrap this tradition completely, or throw one stem or have a smaller replica made instead – it's up to you.

Old, New, Borrowed, Blue

Lots of brides still follow this tradition and it's particularly nice if the items you pick have some meaning, such as a family heirloom. You can go modern with blue nail varnish (on your toes!) or a blue stone added to your tiara or sewn into your dress or stay traditional with a borrowed garter and an old necklace. The rhyme concludes with the line 'and a silver sixpence in her shoe' and it's not as difficult to lay your hands on one of these as you might think! A quick web search or browse through a wedding magazine will find you a list of suppliers or maybe there is a sixpence in the family somewhere, just waiting for you!

The 'Nasty' Tradition

Apparently it's ever so amusing to sneak into the bride and groom's room and 'decorate' it in a humorous fashion. Unfortunately, these little jokes rarely raise a laugh when you are both exhausted at 2am or when you are given a whopping cleaning bill. One way to escape this is to make sure your hotel doesn't give the room key to anyone but the bride under any circumstances. I say 'bride' because people in suits matching the groom can easily be 'confused' with the groom himself but there is usually only one person in a big dress!

Managing Stress

Even the most organised bride might well suffer from a few stressful moments, so if you do feel a little swamped, it's not a reflection on you, just a reminder that planning a wedding can be hard work. Ask for help if you start to feel rather overwhelmed and remember that balancing the wedding organisation with a 'normal' life will help – try not to see the wedding as the end of the experience, because it's simply the beginning of your married life. Becoming consumed by the day will undoubtedly bring you extra stress so use the information and advice in this book and work through everything you need to do logically. Organising your time so that you don't feel like you are continually swimming against the tide is probably the best thing you can do – you need to have time with your partner, your family and your friends because these are the people who will support you and keep you sane.

Tick, tick, tick . . .

However well you have used your time in the months before the wedding, there will be some things you can only do the week before (collecting suits, dropping off items at venues, etc.) so write a very comprehensive list of what needs doing and ask other people to help you out.

* When you pack items to take to your venue, write a list of everything inside the box as you pack it and stick it on the lid. It'll save you unpacking to check things are there and it'll save time on the day when everyone knows where everything is.
* Over-estimate on time for 'little' jobs like writing place cards. These things often take longer than you imagine and you will make fewer mistakes when you are not under time pressure.
* You might not be able to pack for your honeymoon until the day before but make things a bit easier on yourself by buying sun cream and other essentials well in advance so you don't have to find time for a shopping trip too.
* Don't forget food! All the running around in the last week and the 'I've not got time to eat' feeling are the reasons why lots of brides lose weight in the run-up to the wedding (sounds good but isn't when your dress has been fitted). Plan ahead and organise for an on-line shop to be delivered so you have got plenty of quick and healthy food around.
* Do schedule in a bit of 'you' time – either go for a manicure or a swim. You will feel a lot better for it!
* As great as internet wedding discussion forums can be, be wary about spending too much time on them. Reading about a hundred other sets of plans can make you question your own when there is no need to.

CHAPTER CHECKLIST

Hopefully this chapter will have given you plenty to think about. As much as you might dislike me for giving you a seemingly endless list of new things to think about, I promise you that it's better you are aware of everything early on than have it spring on you when you are not expecting it! The key things to remember from this chapter are:

∗ There is no 'perfect wedding recipe' – etiquette and tradition can be followed, twisted or utterly disposed of if you wish. Remember to make it personal and if anyone questions you, you are starting a new family tradition!

∗ Remember that your wedding planning needn't take over your life. Keep a balance and take breaks to spend lots of time with your friends and family.

∗ Ask for help if you feel you need it. Whether you enlist a friend, family member or a professional planner/ co-ordinator is up to you.

∗ Being organised in the run-up to the day will really help manage your stress levels in those final few weeks. Keep a note of what you have done and what needs to be done so you are not worrying that something has been forgotten.

∗ Look after yourself! All the last-minute running around and general excitement can really take it out of you and you do not want a cold for your wedding day. Remember to eat well and get plenty of sleep.

∗ Be wary about spending too much time on wedding forums. Your plans are perfect for you so you can do without feeling as though you need to live up to anyone else's plans.

Seventeen
The Countdown:
Your Priorities

Once the engagement ring is on their finger, most brides can't wait to start planning but it can be tough knowing where to start. In this chapter I've covered what should be top of your priority lists during the run-up to your wedding. It might feel odd making arrangements so far in advance but most venues and suppliers always have bookings for more than 12 months in advance.

* Draw up a budget and decide who'll pay for what.
* Get lots of venue information and visit them.
* Decide on a venue and book it as soon as possible – venues during popular dates can get booked up years in advance.
* Work out how many guests you can invite and draw up a rough guest list.
* Make a provisional booking with your registrar (if they allow it).
* Make an appointment with your registrar to give notice and make a firm booking.
* Start looking through magazines and websites for ideas and suppliers – keep all your ideas in a folder.
* Start thinking about colour schemes or themes.
* Think about who you would like to be your best man,

bridesmaid and other attendants and ask them to make sure they keep that date free.

* Investigate your honeymoon options and think about making a booking if you are looking at somewhere popular in high season.

* Book 'the big ones' – photographer, videographer, caterers, florists, transport providers and entertainers.

* Decide with your photographer before the day how long you want to spend having photographs taken and don't be afraid to say 'enough'. Spending time with your guests is what makes your wedding special.

* If you are planning on having a one-off cake, you should start contacting suppliers now.

* 12 months is not too early to start shopping for a wedding dress – it may take some time to find your dream dress and the order times on some dresses can be longer than you expect. You should start looking for attendants' outfits too.

Your Planning Timeline

To help you, I have listed pointers in this section to help you get organised at crucial times of your planning schedule. If you are feeling very organised and do a few things from the other lists slightly early, it's not a problem. It's better to do things early, especially bookings, and have them out of the way. This helps cut down on stress too and makes budgeting easier as you know your costs earlier on.

Six Months to Go

It's getting closer now! There is a little lull at this point so quite a few brides feel that their plans have stalled a little. Don't worry, the madness is yet to come!

* Decide on your wedding invitations and place your order. It might be a good idea to send out invitations at

this stage if you are worried about people making other plans on your day. It also gives you plenty of time to chase any outstanding replies before you need to give final numbers to your venue and caterers.

✳ Decide on what readings and music you want for your ceremony and check that they are okay with your register office if applicable.

✳ If you are planning on losing weight for your wedding, you should start now.

✳ You should have ordered your dress by this point.

✳ Look at clothes for the men in the party and make any necessary appointments to have them measured.

✳ Book your hotel for the wedding night or make any other necessary arrangements.

✳ Wedding insurance can cover the loss of deposits etc., so it might be wise to look into this now.

✳ Set up a wedding website so you can send the address to guests with your wedding invitations.

✳ Make a decision about your gift list and register your interest with the store concerned – they'll advise you when you need to choose your gifts.

✳ Have a meeting with your florist to discuss your exact requirements.

✳ For a funky first dance, you could book yourselves some lessons or buy a learn-to-dance video.

✳ Buy your wedding underwear and shoes as you will need this for any fittings.

✳ Reserve any accommodation at your venue for guests.

✳ Make a final decision on favours and decorations.

✳ If you are hiring anything such as chairs or table linen, you should book this now.

✳ Start a good beauty regime and book any facials or sunbed sessions.

✳ Make plans for your hen and stag parties.

Three Months to Go

Things are hotting up now so keep an eye on your 'to do' list to make sure everything is in hand. Here is a guide of what needs doing now.

* Finalise your honeymoon plans.
* You can now apply for a passport in your new married name.
* You will also need to apply for any visas or arrange any honeymoon vaccinations.
* Buy your going away clothes and any new bits and pieces you need for your holiday.
* Call your registrar to confirm your booking and to arrange a meeting to go through the ceremony.
* Write any personalised wedding vows if you are thinking about doing this.
* Send your invitations if you haven't already.
* Decide on the food and drink you will be offering and then order menus.
* Print any orders of the day or orders of ceremony that you want.
* Buy your wedding rings.
* Choose wedding gifts for your parents, attendants and for each other!
* Check the bookings for mens' outfits and get any children measured now.
* Start breaking in your wedding shoes.
* Organise a wedding dress fitting.
* Make an appointment with your hairdresser and take along your head-dress if you are having one.

One Month to Go

It's the final countdown now and you are into the stage where you will be arranging all the little details. Remember at this stage to take some time out from wedding planning and spend it as a couple to stop you stressing out.

* Contact any guests who haven't replied to their invitation and make a final list of who'll be attending.
* Give final numbers to your venue so that they can prepare your invoice.
* Write a draft table plan – it's best not to finalise it until a little closer to the date in case people drop out at the last minute.
* Book your final hair, make-up and beauty appointments.
* Meet with your photographer/videographer to run through the details of the day.
* Have a final meeting with your venue to ask any last-minute questions and to double-check your arrangements.
* Enjoy your final dress fitting!
* Go on your stag or hen night (at least one week before the big day).
* Write any speeches that you will be making and practise them.
* Buy a guest book or table cameras.
* Double-check that the names on your passport and travel documents match.
* Call your home insurer if you need to increase your cover to take account of wedding presents and rings.
* Call all your suppliers to confirm all the arrangements you have made.

One Week to Go

Eek! Pre-wedding nerves have probably set in now and you've got that 'headless chicken' feeling. A drop of Bach's Rescue Remedy, available from high-street chemists, can help you out and don't feel that you can't ask people for help if you need it.

* Arrange currency for your honeymoon.
* Decide what you will be taking with you and make sure it's washed and ironed – you can pack toiletries and non-creasing items now.
* Have a final try-on of your entire outfit.
* Wrap the gifts and write the cards for your family and attendants.
* If you need to pay any suppliers on the day, get the cash and put it in labelled envelopes.
* Have a trial run of your journey to the venue so you know how long it should take on the day – you can also check for any planned roadworks, etc.
* Make sure someone can take your dress/car home from the venue.
* Arrange for someone to return all hired clothes to the store after the wedding.
* Make a final seating plan and write place cards.
* Pack everything that needs to be taken to the venue and double-check.
* Have any beauty treatments (waxing, etc.) and the groom should have a final haircut.

One Day Left

Less than 24 hours to go until you are married but there are still a few last-minute things to do.

* Pack the last bits into your honeymoon case.
* If you are staying elsewhere that night, make sure you've got your dress, underwear, shoes, head-dress, bag and any other accessories. You'll also need all your

make-up and clothes for the following morning (if you've got a strapless dress, go bra-less in the morning to avoid the possibility of red marks on your shoulders!)

* Decide in advance what order everyone will be having their hair and make-up done so you don't waste time in the morning when people arrive.
* Pin up a time plan in the room where you are getting ready so everyone can see it. This will save everyone continually asking you questions!
* Lay out your entire outfit the night before. You don't want to be hunting for a shoe or earring just before you need to leave.
* Find out what time suppliers will be arriving – this is especially important if you don't want the photographer to arrive whilst you are still in the shower!
* Make sure the cases will be taken to the reception venue.
* Have a manicure and relax for a few minutes.
* It could be worth treble-checking your arrangements if it will stop you worrying.
* Check who has the rings and that someone will bring home any presents and cards.
* If you are not giving gifts during your speech, you might like to do this today as you will be pushed for time on the day.
* Check your car! If it's getting anyone to the venue, make sure it's got petrol, water and oil!
* Men should clean their shoes thoroughly.
* Try and have an early night so you are fresh the next day – if you can't sleep, don't try alcohol to help you!

On the Day

The day has arrived and you will be fine if you keep the following in mind:

* Make sure someone is keeping an eye on the time. One minute you've got hours to wait and the next, it's time to go so don't get caught out.
* Let someone else keep things on time for you. Delegate the job to a member of the wedding party or hire a co-ordinator to worry about this for you. Making sure dinner, drinks and dances start at the right moment shouldn't be your job when it's your big day.
* Fight the temptation to leave early for the ceremony. It's awful having to drive around because you are early and all your guests haven't arrived. That said, don't aim on being late, especially for a civil ceremony – most registrars do more than one wedding per day and they don't like you being late.
* Spend time with your partner! As crazy as this might seem, it's all too easy to spend your day separate from each other in a whirlwind of speaking to guests, greeting arrivals and generally being the host. Try to make sure you 'make the rounds' together so when you look back on the day and talk about it, you can share the same experiences.

After the Wedding

I bet you thought it was all over didn't you? Well, there are still things that need to be dealt with after the day so don't forget the following:

* Write your thank-you cards. A handwritten thank-you card should be sent to guests as soon as possible. Give yourself a deadline by which to write them and even promise yourself a treat when you've finished the task. Do try to personalise the note a little – it actually

makes writing them less of a chore when you are not repeating the same things over and over.

* Have your gown cleaned and properly stored as soon as possible. Even if you are not going to clean it, it should still be boxed and wrapped in acid-free tissue paper to help preserve it.

* Make sure that all hired formal wear is returned by the specified date. If you are going on honeymoon, make sure that someone returns the groom's outfit because you won't want to return to an overdue charges bill.

* If you were happy with your suppliers, let them know. A card or an e-mail is always lovely to receive and if you are willing to act as a referee, mention that too.

* Don't forget the legal stuff, as boring as it may seem – if you have a will in your maiden name, it becomes null and void upon marriage so schedule an appointment to update it. This is obviously not the most interesting task on the post-wedding list but it's essential and you will feel incredibly responsible once you have done it!

* If you and your husband had a child together before your marriage, you should both re-register the birth to ensure that you both have equal rights in the eyes of the law. You will need to complete Form LA1 which is available from your registry office and you will be issued with a 'new' birth certificate as a result.

* If you were driven, either by chauffeur or a friend, to the airport before you jet off on honeymoon, make arrangements for someone to collect you too! Leave behind your flight number, landing time and terminal details if applicable so you are not left waiting in the arrivals area for too long!

* Videographers will often ask for a choice of music to accompany your film so if you can let them have this before the day, it will mean you get your finished video a lot faster. Similarly, if your photography package

includes an album, making your choice of covers and page colours will allow the album to be ordered before you are even back from honeymoon.

Make Sure You've Told Everyone

And I'm not talking about friends and family. There is a long list of people you will need to contact once you are married, particularly if you are changing your name. Some will require the original marriage certificate, others will be happy with a copy or some will only need a phone call, so check what is required. The companies and organisations you might need to tell are:

* Employer
* Inland Revenue (obtain your reference and address from your employer)
* Department of Health and Social Security (write to the Contributions Agency at your local Social Security Office)
* Local authority (to change council tax and voting records)
* Doctor
* Dentist
* DVLC (for your driving licence and any car registration documents)
* Passport office
* Bank (mortgage, sole and joint accounts, share trading accounts, business accounts)
* Building society (mortgage and/or savings accounts)
* Credit card and store charge-card companies
* Finance/loan companies (cars, household goods, etc.)
* Premium Bond office
* Investment companies
* Companies that you have shares in (the name of the registrars should be on your certificates or paperwork)

* Utilities (gas, electricity, telephone)
* Mobile phone provider
* Veterinary surgery
* Pension provider
* Insurance companies (motor, medical, life, buildings and contents, pets, etc.)
* Mail-order catalogue companies
* Motoring organisations (RAC, AA, etc.)
* Professional institutes and bodies
* Clubs, societies and associations
* Solicitors, financial advisers, etc.
* Internet service provider (if your e-mail address incorporates your old name, you may wish to change your e-mail address)
* Magazine subscriptions

Although this is a rather dull and time-consuming task, it's vital that you do this. In some cases, failure to update your details can be seen as committing an offence (and that's not a good way to start your marriage!).

TAMRYN'S TIP

To make the name-change procedure a little quicker, you can ask your registrar for a copy marriage certificate so you can send an original copy to more than one place at one time. Speak to your registrar about this (there will be a charge for a copy certificate).

CHAPTER CHECKLIST

After reading the lists in this chapter, you should have a much clearer idea of the essentials you need to have covered and when. The most important things to remember are:

✳ Be clever with your time – instead of dashing around to your venue, photographer, florist and other suppliers, try to arrange to meet them all at your venue on the same day. Spread the appointments out and maybe even treat yourselves to lunch and some 'quality time'.

✳ You need to plan the morning of the wedding too. Having lots of people rushing around and continually asking you questions will stop it from being an enjoyable experience.

✳ Confirm with all of your suppliers when they will be arriving on the day. This can save you a lot of worry wondering if people are late when they are probably perfectly on time according to their own schedule.

✳ Before you get married, make an appointment to visit your photographer after your honeymoon to view your photographs. This will give you something to look forward to and they will have a date to work to as well.

✳ The work doesn't stop at the wedding day so don't forget to write your thank-you cards and complete your other post-wedding tasks. Informing banks, employers and other official bodies of your marriage needs to be a priority.

Further Information

I hope that this book has given you plenty of useful information and a great foundation from which you can plan your wedding, whatever style you choose, but it's always great to look around to find out more. Inspiration and information – you can never have too much of either when you are organising a wedding!

Ceremony Information

Links to the websites of a number of denominations that explain more about their wedding services:

www.catholic-ew.org.uk – The Catholic Church in England and Wales
www.cofe.anglican.org/lifeevents/weddings – Church of England
www.gro.gov.uk – The General Register Office (information on civil weddings and much more)
www.humanism.org.uk – The British Humanist Association (weddings and affirmations)
www.jmc-uk.org – The Jewish Marriage Council
www.mcb.org.uk – The Muslim Council of Britain
www.hinducounciluk.org – The Hindu Council

For more ideas on readings and music for the ceremony, take a look at *Wedding Readings and Musical Ideas* by Rev. John Wynburne and Alison Gibbs, published by Foulsham.

Ideas and Details

www.giveit.co.uk – Innovative gift list company that allows guests to donate to charities of your choosing.

www.honeymoney.co.uk – If you don't want wedding gifts but do want a great honeymoon, this could be the answer.

www.mypublisher.com – Fabulous photograph albums that you design yourself. You give them the images, decide on the layout and they print the whole album for you.

www.tkweddings.com – Offers great workshops for brides led by two of the most well-known wedding planners in the UK.

www.weddingideasmagazine.co.uk – Compact monthly magazine, filled to bursting with ideas to suit all budgets.

Planning Resources

www.confetti.co.uk – The UK's biggest wedding website with loads of information, massive supplier directory and useful message boards.

www.hitched.co.uk – Home of the busiest bridal discussion forums in the UK! Be warned, it can be addictive.

www.theknot.com – US-based website with lots of regularly updated articles, features and photo galleries.

www.weddingpath.com – A great website including weblogs, podcasts and a free wedding website builder for everyone.

Professional Bodies

www.flowers.org.uk – The Flowers & Plants Association website has lots of information on wedding flowers, seasonal availability and a list of florists.

www.nabas.co.uk – The Balloon Association gives advice on finding a balloon decorator and things you need to consider. List of member companies included.

www.thempa.com – There are useful tips on wedding photography and photographers on the Master Photographers Association site.

www.ukawp.co.uk – The UK Alliance of Wedding Planners is the place to look if you need help with either the planning or the management of the day.

Speeches

Jarvis, Lee, *Wedding Speeches*, 1993, Foulsham

Jeffrey, Barbara, *Wedding Speeches and Toasts*, 1998, Foulsham

Murray, Mitch, *One-liners for Wedding Speeches*, 1995, Foulsham

Index

Page numbers in **bold** indicate major references.

announcements 89, 165
approved premises 45
artists 158

bags 184
balloons 158–59, 205
bank accounts 28
banns 52
best man 91, 110–11, 123–24, 128
  duties 112–14
  speech **125–26**, 162
best woman 123–24, **232**
blue (colour) 193, 202, **233**
brainstorming **9–14**, 17–19, 131
bridal showers 232
bride
  giving away 226
  name change 246–47
  outfit 24, **176–86**, 196
  speech 125
bridesmaids 61, **118–20**, 129, 226, 230
'bride 's man ' 123–24
budgeting 6–8, 229
  organising a budget 26–8
  sample budget sheet 34–43
  setting a budget 22–6
  who pays? 228–29

cakes **99–102**, 222
  alternatives to 101–02
  cost 25, 100
  cutting 89, 164–65, 228

candles 164, **204–8**
cash bars 227–28
cash gifts 149, 230
casinos 157
caterers 104–7
catering budget 94–5
  see also drinks; food
ceremonies 11, 21–2, 44–5, 225–26, 249
  Church of England 21, **50–4**
  civil 22, **45–50**, 62
  cost 23, 64
  guest involvement 162
  Roman Catholic 54–5
  timing of 91
certificates
  documents to produce 46
  marriage 47, 48, 50, 61
charitable donations 149
chief bridesmaid 110–11, **114–16**
children 92, **134–35**
  entertainment for 159–61
  favours for 208
chocolate fountains 158
church ceremonies
  Church of England 50–4
  marriage classes 50
  permission 52–3
  rehearsing 60–1
  Roman Catholic 54–5
civil ceremonies 22, **45–50**, 62
  cost 64
colours 197–98
common licenses 52
conference centres 68
contracting the marriage 49
contracts (venue) 77–8